Truth
FOR THE
JOURNEY

APMI Publications
a division of Kingdom Dimension Books
P.O. Box 17,
55051 Barga (LU),
Tuscany, Italy

DO YOU SEE THE ELEPHANT IN THE ROOM?

Truth
FOR THE
JOURNEY

A Collection of Dr. Alan's Letters to the Church, with over 90 testimonies from around the world

Dr. Alan Pateman

© 2023 by Alan Pateman

BOOK TITLE:
Truth for the Journey–Letters to the Church

This edition published in 2023

Published by APMI Publications
A Division of Kingdom Dimension Books, Library No. **60**
P.O. Box 17,
55051 Barga (LU),
Italy

Email: publications@alanpatemanworldmissions.com
www.AlanPatemanWorldMissions.com

APMI Publications and Kingdom Dimension Books are a division of Alan Pateman World Missions

Printed in the United States of America, Europe and Asia

All rights reserved under International Copyright Law. Contents and/or cover may not be reproduced in whole or in part in any form without the express written consent of the Publisher.

Paperback ISBN: 978-1-909132-91-7
Hardcover ISBN: 978-1-909132-92-4
eBook ISBN: 978-1-909132-84-9

Acknowledgements:
Author/Design/Senior Editor/Publisher: Apostle Dr. Alan Pateman
Editing/Proofreading/Research: Dr. Jennifer Pateman
Computer Administration/Office Manager: Dr. Dorothea Struhlik
Cover Image Credit: www.PosterMyWall.com

*Where scriptures appear with special emphasis (**in bold**, italic or <u>underlined</u>) we have edited them ourselves in order to bring focused attention within the context of this subject being taught.*

Dedication

I lovingly dedicate this book to all the truth seekers out there who pursue genuine revelation from the Spirit of God's Word.

Letters to the Church

	Introduction	11
1.	We Have Access	15
2.	Death is Conquered, the Victory Secure!	21
3.	We need Never be Denied	25
4.	Our Supernatural "Grace-Thing!"	33
5.	Self-Exaltation Denies Grace	43
6.	The Reality of Righteousness	51
7.	More than Religious Clichés	61
8.	Winning in Life through a Winning Mind	69
9.	Signs of a Renewed Mind	77
10.	Our God Given Antidote to Stress	85
11.	Are You Free or Just Out of Control?	89

12.	We Need to Act	95
13.	Faith to Live By	103
14.	Marginalizing Faith is Not Pro-Active	109
15.	His Faith Alone Can Accomplish	117
16.	Faith Operates by Believing and Saying	123
17.	The Perils of Double Mindedness, Doubt and Unbelief	131
18.	The Perils of Fear	137
19.	The Perils of Disappointment	145
20.	Worry is Practical Atheism	153
21.	Happiness Begins Between Your Ears	157
22.	Every Situation and Circumstance	161
23.	God's X-ray Vision	167
24.	We are the Prophet of our Own Lives!	175
25.	Don't Speak until God Gives you the Key	183
26.	Spirit and Word	189
27.	The Fellowship of the Holy Spirit	199
28.	Cultivating a Deep and Daily Fellowship with the Holy Spirit	209
29.	Biblical Mandate for Fellowship with God's Spirit	219
30.	Can We Talk to the Holy Spirit and Hear His Voice	229
31.	Experience vs. Truth	237
32.	Liberation from Segregation	245
33.	Let's Make the Transition into the 21st Century	251

34.	Traditions of Man make the Word of God of no Effect!	257
35.	Lord, Electrify the Fence!	263
36.	Don't Lose Sight of Honour	271

Introduction

Over the years I've been inspired to send out hundreds of letters to the Church at large, which I'm happy to say, have gone all over the world. Remembering that my heart as an apostolic gift is to teach and train the saints for works of service *(Ephesians 4:12)*. One statement I've always made is that if we can reach the Pastors with revelation and prophetic insight, then it will bring transformation to the body of Christ.

Therefore it has been my privilege to select these 36 letters in order to compile this particular book entitled "Truth for the Journey." We've also included at the back of this book over 90 testimonies from leaders from many different nations, who have given tremendous feedback regarding how these letters have brought change, not only to their lives but also impacted their families and congregations.

It's hard to believe that many of us are bound by our traditions that I've always called *"pillars" (Judges 16:25)*. Samson for example, had been so anointed that the devil had to go to great lengths in order to discover what could successfully weaken him and then place him under perpetual bondage.

According to Judges 16:21 Samson's eyes were *"gouged out"* and he was *"bound"* with *"bronze shackles"* and spent his days, *"grinding grain in the prison" (NIV)*. This meant that Samson's life was no longer fulfilling any kind of destiny and woke daily, only to go round in endless meaningless circles, bound to the wishes of his cruel slave drivers. Deception is so easy, particularly when others are stroking and embracing our egos!

Like the popular idiom suggests, sometimes truth is staring us in the face. Those things we seek are hidden in plain sight! This *"elephant in the room,"* can be so large and looming that we'd have to willfully miss it. Daily we must humbly ask the Lord to open our eyes. Like David said,

> *Show me your ways, Lord, teach me your paths. Guide me in your truth and teach me, for you are God my Saviour and my hope is in you all day long.*
> (Psalm 25:4-5 NIV)

It's God's intention that we walk in the abundance of truth, insight and revelation. Then we are not easily deceived like Samson and others were. God wants us to walk in freedom because He has set us apart, each to fulfill specific tasks. So, what is yours?

Introduction

Who then is the man that fears the Lord? He will instruct him in the way chosen for him. He will spend his days in prosperity, and his descendants will inherit the land.
(Psalm 25:12-13 NIV 1984)

God desires to instruct us in *His* ways that *He* has chosen for us; only then will we spend our lives in prosperity, which in turn will secure a bountiful inheritance and worthy legacy for our children and our children's children.

LETTER 1

Truth for the Journey

We Have Access

Letter to the Church, 13th July 2010

*T**his is how God showed his love among us: He sent his one and only Son into the world that we might live through him.*

(1 John 4:9-10)

The strength of God's love for us was revealed through the price that He was willing to pay - the very blood of His own son Jesus Christ. "Dear friends, let us love one another, for love comes from God. Everyone who loves has been born of God and knows God. Whoever does not love does not know God, because God is love. This is how God showed his love among us: He sent his one and only Son into the world that we might live through him. This is love: not that we loved God, but that he loved us and sent his Son as an atoning sacrifice for our sins" *(1 John 4:7-10)*.

I think it has to be said that the majority of the Body of Christ don't really understand the profound LOVE of God; the Love that took the "divine initiative" of making "reconciliation" with Him possible.

Any love we show Him is just our response to His divine love with which He "first" loved us *(John 3:3, 16; Romans 3:22-26)*. He took the "first step" towards us, through the ultimate act of Love, which was to send His one and only begotten to die as the final atonement for our personal sins. In other words, **Jesus picked up the cheque and the debt has been cleared...!**

The offering up of *Himself* was the ultimate and perfect of all offerings which satisfied the justice of God. Only on the grounds of that sacrifice can God the Father accept us as His own and judge us INNOCENT for all eternity. Jesus died in our place and without Him we were unrighteous and had no hope of ever being righteous outside of the cross. Our only hope was Christ, and He failed us not; He stepped into our place and suffered the penalty that was due us. Without sin, he suffered the punishment of a sinner - the requirement of the law.

RIGHTEOUSNESS TOOK THE PLACE OF UNRIGHTEOUSNESS

Only through Christ can the unrighteous become righteous. Jesus nailed unrighteousness to the cross, and through Him we can be made righteous before God. We can stand "right" in the sight of God.

> *For Christ died for sins once for all, the righteous for the unrighteous, to bring you to God. He was put to death in the body but made alive by the Spirit...*
>
> *(1 Peter 3:18)*

No longer do obstacles stand in the way. After His death on the cross the veil in the temple was torn in two. Any separation that was experienced before the cross is now obliterated through the eternal blood covenant made at Calvary. "But their minds were made dull, for to this day the same veil remains when the Old Covenant is read. It has not been removed, because **only in Christ is it taken away**" *(2 Corinthians 3:14).*

We have ACCESS through the blood, access to the THRONE OF LOVE. Never could we have called God *"FATHER"* without the blood. Only Jesus made reconciliation possible. In fact, every single time salvation occurs for the "individual," instantly the veil is taken away! "**...WHENEVER** anyone turns to the Lord, the veil is taken away. Now the Lord is the Spirit, and where the Spirit of the Lord is, there is freedom" *(2 Corinthians 3:16-17).*

Only when we TURN *(repent)* can the veil be taken from us. In God's sight the washing of the blood has made us CLEAN and now His Spirit has come to live in us, now we can experience true "freedom" by His Spirit. Freedom from the bondages of sin and death, freedom to live "in" Christ and "for" Christ, freedom to be a child of God and freedom to worship Him in "...spirit and in truth" *(John 4:24).*

HIS AMAZING LOVE HAS SET US FREE!

Through Him, death has been conquered and the victory made secure forever. Jesus completely shared our "humanity." Temptation was not far from Him, at any time and still He "never" sinned! Even death He tasted, but not for Himself... In fact He had no reason to die - for Himself - because He was "without sin..." *(2 Corinthians 5:21)*

The only reason Christ died was for the sake of "humanity," who were the rightful recipients of the "death penalty" - because of their sins against God. But Jesus changed everything! "Since the children have flesh and blood, he too shared in their humanity so that by his death he might destroy him who holds the power of death - that is, the devil - and free those who all their lives were held in slavery by their fear of death" *(Hebrews 2:14-15)*.

God's judgement rested upon humanity heavily and could not be averted. Sin had to be punished by death; blood had to be shed, in order to appease the righteousness of God. Jesus satisfied these righteous requirements through dying a *"sinless"* death. Eternal "separation" was to be the verdict passed against humanity - but Jesus appealed on the grounds of His blood and won the case - which will never be overruled! This means that the fear of death has no more power over us - Hallelujah!

It was Isaiah who prophesied Jesus' victory over disease and sickness "This was to fulfil what was spoken through the prophet Isaiah: 'He took up our infirmities and carried our diseases'" *(Matthew 8:17)*. In Matthew chapter 4 verse

24 it says that Jesus healed all who were brought to Him. And during His ministry on earth Jesus demonstrated the Father's love by healing their infirmities. Love desires that no one, "...should perish but have everlasting life" *(John 3:16)*.

The condition of our spirit, soul and body are of importance to God *(1 Thessalonians 5:23)*. Jesus didn't just take our sin to the cross but also our infirmities and diseases; "...by his wounds we are healed" *(Isaiah 53:5)*.

John 4:34 says that Jesus came to do the will of the Father "...to do the will of Him who sent me..." It is the Father's will that we be saved, healed and receive every spiritual blessing *(see Ephesians 1:3-14)*. And Jesus did all that was necessary to see that this was fulfilled, "...and to finish His work." That's why Jesus could declare from the cross before he died, "It is FINISHED..." *(John 19:30)* And that's why today, those of us who are "in" Christ can rest secure that "spirit, soul & body," the work of the cross, is "complete!"

ENDNOTES:

1. This "Truth for the Journey" has been taken from: https://watchersofthe4kings.com
2. Scripture references are taken from the HOLY BIBLE, NEW INTERNATIONAL VERSION ®. NIV ®. Copyright © 1973, 1978, 1984 by the International Bible Society. Used by permission of Zondervan Publishing House. All rights reserved.

LETTER 2

Truth for the Journey

Death is Conquered, the Victory Secure!

Letter to the Church, 2nd April 2010

*B*ecause God's children are human beings-made of flesh and blood-the Son also became flesh and blood. For only as a human being could he die, and only by dying could he break the power of the devil, who had the power of death. Only in this way could he set free all who have lived their lives as slaves to the fear of dying.
(Hebrews 2:14-15 NLT)

Jesus shared our humanity completely. Temptation was not far from him and yet he never sinned. Death he tasted, but not for Himself... In fact he had no reason to die because He was "without sin..." *(2 Corinthians 5:21)* The only reason

Christ died was for the sake of humanity. God's judgement rested upon humanity heavily and could not be averted. Sin had to be punished by death; blood had to be shed, in order to appease the righteousness of God. Jesus satisfied that requirement through dying a "sinless" death.

Eternal separation - was the verdict passed against humanity - but Jesus appealed on the grounds of His blood and won the case - which will never be overturned! Therefore the fear of death has no more power over us and infirmity no longer a foot hold.

Isaiah prophesied Jesus' victory over disease and sickness, "He Himself took [in order to carry away] our weaknesses and infirmities and bore away our diseases" *(Matthew 8:17 AMPC).*

In Matthew chapter 4 verse 24 it says that Jesus healed all who were brought to Him. The condition of our spirit, soul and body are of importance to God *(1 Thessalonians 5:23).* Jesus took our sin to the cross but also our infirmities and diseases "...by his wounds we are healed" *(Isaiah 53:5).*

John 4:34 says that Jesus came to do the will of the Father "...to do the will of Him who sent me..." and it is the Father's will for us to be saved, healed and receive every spiritual blessing *(Ephesians 1:3-14).* Because of this, Jesus did all that was necessary to see His Father's will accomplished; even declaring from the cross, *"It is finished..." (John 19:30)*

The work of the cross is complete. Jesus has risen for us. When all was accomplished, Jesus ascended to His Father's side. But not to close His work! It continues still. He lives forever to minister in the presence of God on our behalf, interceding for us continually, "Who is there to condemn [us]? Will Christ Jesus *(the Messiah)*, Who died, or rather Who was raised from the dead, *Who is at the right hand of God actually pleading as He intercedes for us?" (Romans 8:34 AMPC)*

CAN ANYTHING EVER SEPARATE US FROM CHRIST'S LOVE?

And when God the Father sees Jesus He also sees us, because we are "...seated in heavenly places in Christ Jesus" *(Ephesians 2:6)*. Moreover each time He sees us He should see Christ! We have been reconciled; there is no longer any separation. Does it mean He no longer loves us if we have trouble or calamity, or are persecuted, or hungry, or destitute, or in danger, or threatened with death? "*(As the Scriptures say, 'For your sake we are killed every day; we are being slaughtered like sheep.')* "No, despite all these things, overwhelming victory is ours through Christ, who loved us" *(Romans 8:36-37 NLT)*.

Therefore God the Father always sees us TOGETHER! Under the blood, nothing can separate us! When He looks upon us, He not only sees Christ but also covenant. And if Christ is continually before the Father interceding, then technically so are we! Because we are IN CHRIST JESUS!

That's why in Romans 8:1 it says that the only ones who are free from condemnation are those who are IN CHRIST JESUS. Sadly those who are living in condemnation *(flesh)* cannot stand before the throne of God. It is only those who are IN CHRIST JESUS and who are living "*...according to the Spirit*" that can stand fearless before God.

Take some time to pause and calmly think about what is being said here, *("selah" measure, weigh up)*. Outside of Christ we used to look like sin but now we are in Christ we no longer look like sin - before the Father we actually look like Jesus!

ENDNOTES:

1. This "Truth for the Journey" has been taken from: https://watchersofthe4kings.com

2. Unless otherwise indicated, all scripture references are taken from the HOLY BIBLE, NEW INTERNATIONAL VERSION ®. NIV ®. Copyright © 1973, 1978, 1984 by the International Bible Society. Used by permission of Zondervan Publishing House. All rights reserved.

3. Scripture references marked AMPC are taken from the Amplified® Bible (AMPC), Copyright © 1954, 1958, 1962, 1964, 1965, 1987 by The Lockman Foundation. Used by permission. www.Lockman.org

4. Scripture quotations marked NLT are taken from the Holy Bible, New Living Translation, copyright © 1996, 2004, 2007 by Tyndale House Foundation. Used by permission of Tyndale House Publishers, Inc., Carol Stream, Illinois 60188. All rights reserved.

Letter 3

Truth for the Journey

We need Never be Denied

Letter to the Church, 10th July 2010

> *Wherefore he is able also to save them to the uttermost that come unto God by him, seeing he ever liveth to make intercession for them.*
> *(Hebrews 7:25)*

According to Hebrews 7:25 **Jesus is our faithful High Priest,** who "...ever lives to make intercession for us," and because of this we will never be denied when we enter into God's presence bearing His name! This free passage and unlimited access to God's throne was granted us through the work of the cross, but is **based on the condition that we remain "in" Him.**

Jesus underwent such terrible suffering for a "special" purpose and that was to make us holy, as He is holy *(1 Peter 1:16)*. A sheer impossibility without the "spilling" of the cross "...Jesus...suffered...to make the people holy through his own blood" *(Hebrews 13:12 NIV)*. Because God is the same yesterday, today and forever, and there is no shadow of turning with Him, He is "unable" to change. His love remains constant throughout the generations.

Most importantly because we saw how Jesus remained utterly faithful to His Father's will, throughout every trial and temptation - it is by this we know that without fail or compromise Jesus will remain faithful to us. His faithfulness that has been tried, tested and proven! Making His love for us unfailing, unadulterated and unconditional!

Divine LOVE is never based on anything we are but on who He is; 1 John 4:7-21 says, "God is Love..." and 1 Corinthians 13:8 tells us that "...Love never fails." God's love for us is unaffected by anything we have done or accomplished in our lifetime. Rather it is affected only by what Jesus has done. "I think that if there could be one sight more wonderful than the love of Christ," says Spurgeon, "it would be the blood of Christ..." and continued, "much we talk of Jesus' blood, but how little's understood!"[1]

He further addressed the blood by saying, "I do not know of anything more divine. It seems to me as if all the eternal purposes worked up to the blood of the Cross, and then worked from the blood of the cross towards the sublime consummation of all things. Oh, to think that He should become man! God has made spirit, pure spirit, embodied spirit; and then materialism; and somehow, as if He would take all up into one, the Godhead links Himself with the material. He then wears dust about Him even as we wear it; and taking it all up, He then goes, and in that fashion, redeems His people from all the evil of their soul, their spirit, and their body, by the pouring out of a life, which while it was human, was so in connection with the divine, that we speak correctly of 'the blood of God.'"

When we turn to the twentieth chapter of the book of Acts we find that Paul put it like this, "Feed the church of God, which he hath purchased with his own blood" *(Acts 20:28)*. As a result whenever we hear God addressed as the, "God who loved and died," it could be said that this is an "incorrect accuracy" or like Spurgeon classically coined it, **"a strictly absolute accuracy of incorrectness!"**

Always the case whenever the "finite" tries to talk of the "infinite." When "earthy" try to describe the "heavenly!" Such as the only sacrifice that could ever obliterate, annihilate, and extinguish sin or any trace of it! "He hath finished the transgression, made an end of sins, made reconciliation for iniquity, and brought in everlasting righteousness" *(see Daniel 9:24)*.

When we get to heaven, perhaps only then shall we understand in its entirety just what the blood truly meant. When we see the One who loves us and washed us from our sins in his own blood! May the Holy Spirit show us Gethsemane, Gabbatha, and Golgotha! And show us what our Lord is doing in this precise moment! So that in those times of complete depression we will know that He is standing and pleading for us!

IT'S ALL GOING TO BE OKAY!

In the moment that a family member is ill, *(children or spouse)* and no food is in the cupboards, the pressure is all around but we are able to "see" Christ standing there, dressed in His glory, knowing our name and pleading for us; we could turn to our families and to the circumstances and holler, "He is praying for us, it's all going to be okay!" The sight of Christ praying, pleading and interceding brings courage to swell in the heart - the Holy Spirit must be allowed to show us a pleading Christ!

Nevertheless although He is "pleading" He is still "reigning" at the right hand side of God, where the Father has put "all" things under His feet. No fear exists for those who believe His great declaration, "All power is given unto me in heaven and in earth. Go ye therefore, and teach all nations; and lo, I am with you always, even unto the end of the world" *(see Matthew 28:18-20).*

Most precious of all may the Holy Spirit grant us a clear view of His return. Jesus is "coming," our most brilliant hope! Yet although our adversary behaves even bolder and passionate faith seems almost extinct, these are just "tokens" of His "coming." Even Jesus said that He would not return unless first there was a "falling-away."

So despite the consequences of the growing darkness, we must remind ourselves that on the lake of Galilee Jesus came in the thick of night when the storm was at its worst, to be with His disciples. And just as the storm fled so will the enemies of His Word, name and blood, flee from the face of His "injured love!" As for us, we will stand victorious with the infinite mercy of our loving saviour; seeing with the "natural eye" what the Holy Spirit has been showing us all along!

So it is with divine purpose that the Holy Spirit takes of the things of Christ and shows them unto us. Just as with Jacob who laid himself down to sleep and the Lord began to speak with him, "The land whereon thou liest, to thee will I give it" *(Genesis 28:13)*. We need to ask ourselves this question: Can I sleep on the "promise" of God? Can I relax and trust what He is saying to me without trying to work it out for myself? If yes, the same promise we "sleep-on" is ours! Because being able to "rest" in what God shows us is vitally important and affects whether we become recipients or just observers!

WITHOUT FAITH WE CANNOT SEE!

Consider Abraham, who also heard God say, "Look from the place where thou are northward, and southward, and eastward, and westward: for all the land, which thou seest, to thee will I give it" *(Genesis 13:14-15)*. Effectively God was saying to Abraham, "What you are 'able' to 'see' by faith, I am 'able' give you!" Consequently our ability to "see" is also crucial to our "receiving." Without faith we cannot "see" what God sees. Natural sight limits our scope and hope for the future to "all-things-temporal." Faith which sees what the natural eye can't, engages with God in a way "flesh" can't. We must live by faith and not by *(natural)* sight.

For instance whenever we discovered that we are in a difficult circumstance, it took "seeing" our way out - before it actually happened! We "saw" our deliverance before deliverance showed up, which is faith. Just like the joy that was set "before" Jesus so that He could endure the cross. He "saw" victory before there was victory!

In life we set goals for ourselves, like losing weight or climbing a mountain! We have to see the top, the finish line or even the new thinner self - to keep the incentive alive! But it is still "faith" that achieves this! Without "seeing" the result and keeping it in our "mind's-eye" so to speak - then we don't stay fixed on the goal and therefore never overcome. However the moral of the story is... that in Christ we were born to overcome and what we "see" by faith we can have!

Precisely the reason why God showed both Abraham and Jacob exactly what He wanted them to possess! *(God does not show us anything He does not want us to own - what's the point?!)* On the other hand our adversary torments us "all" the time by showing us what we don't want to have. It's like faith in reverse! But is called fear.

With God He only ever shows us what He wants us to have, therefore if we see what He sees, we can have it! Faith always sees what happens before it happens, so that we can align with it. Living in "agreement" with the vision is the purpose of foreseeing it; whereas "di-vision" is living in "dis-agreement" with the vision, resisting it and making it unproductive. **In other words nothing happens that should happen because faith has been denied.** In fact scripture tells us that the "just shall live by faith" because without it we can't live "for" God or "with" God. He is a faith God; only faith pleases Him because without it we will fail.

Finally, in order for us to be productive *(fruit bearing not barren)* we must be able to "see" daily what God is showing us, because this is what He wants us to have! **We must always permit His Spirit to increase our vision** *(spiritual sight)* **so that we can enjoy all that has been prepared for us in Christ!**

ENDNOTES:

1. Excerpts taken from "Honey in the Mouth!" by C.H. Spurgeon. (No. 2213) A Sermon intended for reading on the Lord's Day (July 19th- 1891), at the Conference of the Pastor's College Evangelical Association. www.ccel.org/ccel/spurgeon/sermons37.xxxii.html

2. This "Truth for the Journey" has been taken from: https://watchersofthe4kings.com

3. Unless otherwise indicated, all scripture references are taken from the King James Version of the Bible.

4. Scripture references marked NIV are taken from the HOLY BIBLE, NEW INTERNATIONAL VERSION ®. NIV ®. Copyright © 1973, 1978, 1984 by the International Bible Society. Used by permission of Zondervan Publishing House. All rights reserved.

Letter 4

Truth for the Journey

Our Supernatural "Grace-Thing!"

Letter to the Church, 10th September 2010

Yet grace (God's unmerited favor) was given to each of us individually [not indiscriminately, but in different ways] in proportion to the measure of Christ's [rich and bounteous] gift.

(Ephesians 4:7 AMPC)

There is much attention given to this subject of Grace; it gets different types of press: good, bad, indifferent and confused! So let's investigate it a little and focus more on what grace IS rather than what grace is not! Let's start with the fact that the death and resurrection of **Jesus Christ altered mankind's relationship with God forever.** It was grace that caused God to make a personal sacrifice and then offer the "fruit" of that sacrifice directly to us! This makes grace much more than a mere "free-gift" and can be defined by using this simple illustration.

Let's just say that one day while minding our own business someone came up to us and pushed something into our hands saying, *"Here are the keys to my Rolls Royce!"* This would be a pretty large gift to most people! BUT let's also say that our normal circumstances meant that we could already purchase this gift if we had chosen to, making the Rolls Royce - a handsome "gift" - but NOT a "gift of grace." On the other hand when it is totally "impossible" for us to obtain this type of "gift" through our own efforts, only then it can be considered a *"gift of grace"* with no possible way of returning the favour. Then all that is left to say is *"Thank you,"* and accept the gift!

THERE IS ONLY ONE WAY TO GOD

What this illustrates mostly is that we can never "earn" grace! If God had not given us salvation, could we have obtained it any other way? *No, impossible!* This is why **Jesus said, "I am the way, and the truth, and the life, no one doth come unto the Father, if not through me"** *(John 14:6 YLT).*

There are no alternatives! If salvation was possible by any other means other than "grace," then perhaps "Krishna's" idea, that there are "many" ways to God, could be true and then several world religions would work! But according to the bible there is only "one" way to God. His name is Jesus of Nazareth. His death and resurrection alone have made "grace" available to us.

Our Supernatural "Grace-Thing!"

This covers more than "forgiveness" of sins and the "new birth," *(when we were "born again" and became Christians),* the same applies to whatever we receive from God - it is by grace. This means that when He gives something to us by grace - we don't receive the glory for it and nor does He have to override our free will to give it to us. It is only possible to receive such a free gift of grace by faith: not of ourselves; "...it is a gift of God: Not of works, least anyone should boast. For we are His workmanship, created in Christ Jesus unto good works, which God hath before ordained that we should walk in them" *(Ephesians 2:8-10).*

Grace can be seen as undeserved and supernatural favour as in the Old Testament Joseph was someone who experienced "supernatural" favour; "But the LORD was with Joseph, and showed him mercy, and gave him favor *(chên)* in the sight of the keeper of the prison" *(Genesis 39:21).*

This tiny Hebrew word *chên (pronounced khane);* #H2580 in Strong's Exhaustive Concordance; fundamentally means graciousness, kindness, favour, beauty, pleasant, precious. And then in close relation the word *chânan (pronounced khawnan)* means; to bend or stoop in kindness to an inferior; to show favour and to have mercy.[1]

However grace is much more than this of course especially in the New Testament. But first we must look in the Old Testament where *chên,* "favour," is the unmerited favour of a superior to an inferior. In the case of God to man; *chên* is demonstrated usually in temporal, though also occasionally in spiritual blessings; within deliverance in both physical and spiritual senses *(Jeremiah 31:2; Exodus 33:19).*

Also in the Old Testament *chêsêd;* "Loving-Kindness," is the firm loving-kindness expressed between related people and particularly in the covenants into which God entered with His people and which His *chêsêd* firmly guaranteed *(2 Samuel 7:15; Exodus 20:6).* "But my mercy *(chêsêd)* shall not depart away from him, as I took it from Saul, whom I put away before thee" *(2 Samuel 7:15).*

MOVING ON INTO THE NEW TESTAMENT

Greek literature gave *charis* the following meanings:

- One that causes attractiveness, such as grace of appearance or speech.
- Favourable regard felt toward a person.
- A favour.
- Gratitude.
- It was used adverbially in phrases such as "for the sake of a thing," *charin tinos.*

This little Greek word χάρις *charis (pronounced khar'-ece),* used in the New Testament "...the law was given by Moses, but grace *(charis)* and truth came by Jesus Christ" *(John 1:17)* Strong's #G5485 "graciousness - divine influence upon the heart, and its reflection in the life; gratitude, acceptable, benefit, favour, gift, grace, joy, liberality, pleasure, thankworthy."[2]

Although it was not until the coming of Christ that grace took on its fullest meaning. His self-sacrifice was grace itself *(2 Corinthians 8:9)* and absolutely free *(Romans 6:14; 5:15-18; Ephesians 1:7; 2:8-9).* When it is received by the believer, it governs his or her spiritual life by compounding favour upon favour. It equips, strengthens, and controls all phases of the believer's life *(2 Corinthians 8:6-7; Colossians 4:6; 2 Thessalonians 2:16; 2 Timothy 2:1)*. Consequently, the Christian gives thanks *(charis)* to God for the riches of grace in His unspeakable gift *(2 Corinthians 9:15)*.

The Apostle Paul was the principal human instrument to convey the fullest meaning of grace in Christ. The New Testament offers grace to all, in contrast to the Old Testament, which generally restricted grace to God's elect people Israel. **Grace in its fullest definition is "God's unmerited favor in the gift of His Son, who offers salvation to all and who gives to all those who receive Him as their personal Saviour, added grace for this life and hope for the future."**

Important to remember is that God's sovereign grace is not arbitrary *(random or by chance)*. In order to "receive it," man must "believe." **In order to "enjoy it," the believer must be "obedient."** Grace also provides the following: acceptance *(Romans 3:24)*, enablement *(Colossians 1:29)*, a new position *(1 Peter 2:5, 9)*, and an inheritance *(Ephesians 1:3, 14)*.

Then at least three motives are indicated in the New Testament as to why God "acts" in grace, especially in salvation. He does it to: express His love *(Ephesians 2:4; John 3:16)*, to display His grace in the ages to come *(Ephesians 2:7)*, and so that redeemed man will produce good works *(Ephesians 2:10)*. This concludes that sovereign grace is always purposeful; the life that is "under grace" is a life of good works.

THERE IS NO NEED FOR SELF-EFFORT

I want to quote Ulf Ekman from his book **"Doctrine"** which is very fitting here: "Man now enjoys a position in Christ before God as though he had never transgressed. He has no sense of guilt, shame or lack, only an overwhelming consciousness of having 'come home,' along with gratitude and love for Jesus, who has so graciously done it all for him.

Since God has accomplished this in Christ Jesus, it is a matter of grace, rather than self-effort. Man has nothing of which he can boast. **Those things in which he does boast are his cardinal sins** - pride, personal achievement, self-importance and rebellion toward God's ways. **Every route to self-exaltation and 'self-salvation' for man is effectively sealed!**

No grounds for bartering exist between him and God where God must do His part and man his. No, it is all God's work! God took the initiative, He made the plans, He initiated them and completed them. God saved man, who was deep in sin, without his suggestions, efforts or help at all.

Salvation is entirely due to God's grace. No religious, idealistic, political or philosophical ideas or deeds will take you to God. No rituals, ceremonies, pilgrimages, fasts, donations or other so called good deeds or religious habits will bring you nearer to Him.

God will only accept your admission that you can do nothing, that you are **spiritually bankrupt.** Then, as you receive by faith, His gift, His grace and all that He has done for you in Christ Jesus, you will be saved. Your sins will be forgiven as you are cleansed in the blood of Jesus. Then the Spirit of God will come to you and you will be born again. You will become a child of God and find peace with Him."[3]

Paul wrote, "...know that a man is not justified by observing the law, but by faith in Jesus Christ. So we, too, have put our faith in Christ Jesus that we may be justified by faith in Christ and not by observing the law, because observing the law no-one will be justified" *(Galatians 2:16 NIV).*

We have discovered the grace of God is so much more than mere *charis* and is sourced both in God the Father and in His Son, Jesus *(Romans 5:15; 1 Corinthians 1:12; Galatians 1:3, 6; 2 Thessalonians 1:12)* and therefore we must reject any confidence that we may have in ourselves, recognising that we are incapable of pleasing God on our own and must entrust ourselves completely to Him.

On the other hand grace is "active" and is what we need in order to "operate" in God, with God and for Him. As Paul wrote to Timothy;

> *I would remind you to stir up (rekindle the embers of, fan the flame of, and keep burning) the [gracious] gift of God, [the inner fire] that is in you by means of the laying on of my hands...*
>
> *(2 Timothy 1:6 AMPC)*

Something we must prize and value because this grace *(call or gift)* of God should be the motivation power for our whole life and work. **We are saved by grace and called into**

grace. Grace is more than particular gifts of the Spirit; it is more like the hand of God coming upon someone's life to single them out for the particular work or area of ministry.

EXPRESSION OR MANIFESTATION OF THE GRACE

Finally, we may have looked at *charis* but the word for "gift" is *charisma*... and these two words come from one another: *charis* meaning "grace" and *ma* meaning "thing;" literally translating not merely as "gift" but as "grace thing" or "thing of grace!"

So when the New Testament talks about "spiritual gifts" it is talking about the "expression or manifestation" of the grace of God in our lives. Now on the other hand there is *charismata,* which is plural for *charisma,* which are the gifts of the Holy Spirit to the entire body of Christ, and made available to each and every member. We could call them "body-gifts" and these are manifested through specific or chosen individuals as the Spirit determines - as seen in 1 Corinthians 12:7, 11. These gifts operate occasionally and are used to meet specific needs as the Spirit directs.

We see this again in 1 Peter,

> *As each of you has received a gift (a particular spiritual talent, a gracious divine endowment), employ it for one another as [befits] good trustees of God's many-sided grace [faithful stewards of the extremely diverse powers and gifts granted to Christians by unmerited favor].*
> (1 Peter 4:10 AMPC)

Our Supernatural "Grace-Thing!"

To close, every believer needs to be open to these "gifts" of the Holy Spirit in their lives and learn how to operate in the power and authority of these gifts. Because we are not only "called BY grace" and "called INTO grace," just as we see that Paul the apostle was not only given "grace" but specifically given "a grace" with which his whole life was controlled and directed. Not by mere graciousness *(charis)* but by *(charis-ma)* the "authority" of that grace *(specific gift, grace-thing)* given him by God.

This applies to us. **We must constantly submit our lives to the grace of God. Not just the divine favour of God over our lives but also to His choice of gifting - grace thing - that He chose for us to "operate" in.** Grace is oftentimes made synonymous with "we can do whatever we want and get away with it" but of course this is erroneous.

Yes! Grace is favour but it is also the power and authority to "operate in obedience" to God.

TRUTH FOR THE JOURNEY

ENDNOTES:

1. Strong, James. S.T.D., L.L.D. 1890. Strong's Exhaustive Concordance, Dictionaries (Lexicon) of the Hebrew and Greek Words

2. Ibid

3. "Doctrine" by Ulf Ekman (pages 185-186) Published by Word of Life Publications, Uppsala, Sweden. Original Swedish edition, copyright © 1995, English translation, copyright © 1996

4. This "Truth for the Journey" has been taken from: https://watchersofthe4kings.com

5. Unless otherwise indicated, all scripture references are taken from the King James Version of the Bible.

6. Scripture references marked AMPC are taken from the Amplified® Bible (AMPC), Copyright © 1954, 1958, 1962, 1964, 1965, 1987 by The Lockman Foundation. Used by permission. www.Lockman.org

7. Scripture references marked NIV are taken from the HOLY BIBLE, NEW INTERNATIONAL VERSION ®. NIV ®. Copyright © 1973, 1978, 1984 by the International Bible Society. Used by permission of Zondervan Publishing House. All rights reserved.

8. Scripture quotations marked YLT are taken from the Young's Literal Translation of the Bible.

Letter 5

Truth for the Journey

Self-Exaltation Denies Grace

Letter to the Church, 14th September 2010

Does that mean we can live any old way we want? ...can we do anything that comes to mind? ...some acts of so-called freedom... destroy freedom... at one time the more you did just what you felt like doing... the worse your life became and the less freedom you had... And how much different is it now as you live in God's freedom, your lives healed and expansive in holiness?
(Romans 6:15-19 MSG)

In the previous Truth for the Journey we looked at grace and what it meant, from salvation onwards. Now we must move on from mere salvation and continue our journey. **It is important to acknowledge that grace "empowers"**

not "pacifies!" Grace enables us to do what we are called to do and not just to sit on our morals thinking that we are exhausting the true purpose of grace!

Grace means change; moving on towards holiness and righteous living as the above scripture states, **"How different is it now** as you live in God's freedom, **healed... and expansive in holiness..."** *(verse 19)* When God really touches our lives with His grace – there is change – everything is **"...different, healed and holy!"**

However as much as we have been given grace and are living by grace – we all still crave the things of the flesh, our fallen nature; sin and the world. Some Christians – even leaders – are ambitious and willingly usurp *(takeover, dominate)* the lives of others as they try and forge out a ministry for themselves; based upon a cocktail of selfish-ambition and what they think they learnt at bible school.

Not upon "divine impartation" or "divine patterns" from heaven *(see Hebrews 9:23; 8:5; Exodus 25:40; 26:30)*. Instead they need to lose their "ambition" and "text-book" approach; humble themselves before God to receive "revelation" by the Spirit, as Moses received his divine instruction and pattern on the mountain. There is no basis for anything without this! No matter how much research we do and I am somebody who certainly values study – but not without the Spirit. Without Him all study is "dead-letter." In fact anything is dead without Him breathing on it.

Then on the other hand there are some folks who are just so "relaxed" about grace – they think that it's like the cream between the sponge cakes – that softens every blow! However they fundamentally misunderstand the purpose of grace. Grace is to go "through" *(not escape!)* to overcome and to thrive *(not just dwell and survive!)* Grace always works hand in hand with faith; not fear. "Playing-things-safe" does nothing for God!

CALL YOURSELF A GRACE-JUNKIE?

Then there are those who like to call themselves "grace-junkies" and I am okay with this in the context that we all need to be craving more of God's grace every single day - but grace is not a means to sin. It is a means to "live" for God. Grace is not even a means to escape conviction. For if we harden our hearts to the Holy Spirit's conviction in our lives – we eventually fall into sin anyway.

The grace lifestyle is different to grace just for salvation. **We all need grace for salvation but we also need the grace lifestyle that takes us onto "maturity" and "effectiveness" for God.** This includes purity and holiness.

> Ephesians 2:7-10 *(KJV)* says *"...the exceeding riches of his grace in his kindness toward us through Christ Jesus. For by grace are ye saved through faith; and that not of yourselves: it is the gift of God: Not of works, lest any man should boast. For we are his workmanship,* **created in Christ Jesus unto good works, which God hath before ordained that we should walk in them..."**

My emphasis here is not *(grace for)* salvation but that we have a job to do! Good works ordained by God that we should walk in them. Not living-it-up in the largest church we can find; enjoying the best worship available so we can "celebrate" the fact that we are saved each and every week but do nothing with it! This is not being "active" for God! This is still all about "self."

RECEIVING A PATTERN FROM HEAVEN

However God **"ordained" good works for us to do and this requires both forces of grace and faith to accomplish it. Passively "accepting" truth is not "living" truth.** However once we start living in obedience we find this triggers obedience in others. *(Rebellion might seem "contagious" ...but that's just fallen nature already prevalent in all of us from birth... what child ever needs to learn disobedience?! It's inherent in fallen nature...* ***all flesh is corrupt without Christ and is hard-wired to sin!****)* We see this in the book of Revelations, that our testimony of faith and obedience also helps others to overcome *(see 12:11).*

When we talk of receiving a "pattern from heaven" this is something that is available for all of us and we call this God's "job-description" for our lives, but this can only be received by faith. However there are many who are content with just pew-filling and have no intention of receiving any mandate from God. Their only interest is "spectator-sport!" The only grace they want to receive is for salvation, but they are mistaken, because although grace can never be earned - it still must be worked! And faith without the works of grace is dead.

In order to receive this pattern from heaven we must believe and trust the Giver of the pattern; the vision, the blue print – that paints a picture for our future. Faith alone is how we receive it – because faith is the "substance" of things hoped for *(Hebrews 11:1 KJV).*

All this is the work of grace and to continually walk in grace we have to continually humble ourselves; yielding our lives to His will rather than our own - submitting to the things of the Holy Spirit. Therefore in this life we need to hear God – His grace, His pattern and His direction. Believing and trusting Him and acting upon His Word and being obedient to His will. We need to walk by His Word and in His Word. In other words a lifestyle that "reveals" salvation and sanctification. A walk of righteousness and holiness, and in subsequent Truth for the Journeys we will be taking a look at the subject of "righteousness."

We should no longer live a life where we expect God to bless "anything" we do regardless. In such an existence – repentance is not considered necessary! After-all we are saved by grace and He knows all things anyhow! Listen, when repentance is no longer deemed "necessary" – neither is the cross *(God forbid!)*

There are people today who are intimidated to talk about "repentance," because that might suggest that someone is "in" sin! In some circles it is almost a dirty word! How ridiculous. Let me just affirm that if there is no longer any sin – as the psychologists of the world would have us believe – then where is the need for grace? Yet grace is necessary and so is repentance; there are some in the Body of Christ right now who are teaching grace in error. They don't think so of course. But then again the ditches on either side of the truth are very easy to fall into. You get out of one and fall into another; for example: legalism vs. abandonment / hard vs. soft grace – both can be erroneous. Grace is a free *(unearned gift)* but still must be worked by faith.

Besides the only people who benefit from the cross are those who recognise their sin and their need for repentance and salvation. Jesus said from the cross: "Father forgive them for they don't know what they do" *(Luke 23:34)*. Those He was referring to did not understand but this did not reduce their need for "forgiveness!" Sin is sin. Call it for what it is; as Jesus did.

There is nothing polite about it! And there will be nothing polite about it on judgment day; but let's not forget that God's Word already judges us! And if we live according to His Word, as our plumb-line for everyday living – yes we shall be saved - but we will also "live" by holy standards and not by double standards! In addition, it's not hard to see that stretching grace to its limits only encourages "hypocrisy" – which in itself is sin *(Romans 6:16-19)*.

REPENTANCE THAT LEADS TO PURITY

Therefore grace should be presented as a teaching on repentance that leads to purity *(lifestyle)* but is rather presented as a license for immorality and continuing in our sinful natures - with no repentance required. Something that is certainly not new or unique! This began some 2000 years ago in the early church:

For there are certain men who have crept in unnoticed, whose condemnation was predicted long ago, ungodly

> *men, who turn the GRACE of our God into lawlessness and wantonness, a license for immorality; and deny and disown our only Master and Lord Jesus Christ...*
>
> *(Jude 1:4)*

If any sense of guilt is taken away – this only makes it easier for people to sin and feel justified about it! And all the time we justify our actions or our sin; God cannot help us deal with it as we should. We still need God to point out our sin today. We still need the conviction of the Holy Spirit today. We are not trophy winners for just showing up! We are more than conquerors because of Christ, but this thing does not stop with His free gift. It only "begins" there...!

SELF-EXALTATION ONLY LIFTS UP "SELF"

Also in our opening title it says that grace can be "denied," in fact all rebellion "denies" God and it was while I was writing the last Truth for the Journey that I felt God tell me that **"self-exaltation denies grace."** Instead of lifting up Christ, self-exaltation only lifts up "self" and in such lives where is the need for Christ? In fact there are many today who live double-lives; they have a church existence and a worldly-existence, they think that they can go on like this; spiritually co-habiting with themselves! But there is "one life" in Christ.

God cannot bless disobedience even if we are saved. Sure - it is possible to be "saved" by grace yet still not "live" by grace. Many people don't understand this and fail to see that grace empowers them to live the life of "obedience" not "relaxed" Christianity!

To finish, if we are not walking in obedience, we are not really "in" grace or walking "by" grace. Many are living "natural" lives trying to make things work for them. In such cases the role of the Holy Spirit is made obsolete!

Remember His rightful role is to "lead" – not vice-versa; regardless of circumstances. Today we tend to want everything "now" and we throw spiritual tantrums if God does not give us what we want, when we want it – NOW – we have become like spoilt children!

Yet the grace lifestyle is what we all need; conscious of holiness and purity before God our Saviour – we are not just pictures on a wall, waiting to be admired, we are active members of the Body "proving" salvation to the world through our lifestyle - rather than "disproving" it – through our non-existent lifestyle.

ENDNOTES:

1. This "Truth for the Journey" has been taken from: https://watchersofthe4kings.com
2. Scripture references marked KJV are taken from the King James Version of the Bible.
3. Scripture quotations marked MSG are taken from The Message. Copyright © 1993, 1994, 1995, 1996, 2000, 2001, 2002. Used by permission of NavPress Publishing Group.

LETTER 6

Truth for the Journey

The Reality of Righteousness

Letter to the Church, 17th September 2010

*F*or *everyone has sinned...Yet God, with undeserved kindness, declares that we are righteous.*
(Romans 3:23-24 NLT)

We read in Romans chapter 3, beginning with verse 20, "Therefore by the deeds of the law there shall no flesh be justified *(lit. declared righteous),* in his sight; for by the law is the knowledge of sin." Then it goes on to say, "But now God has shown us a way to be made right with him without keeping the requirements of the law, as was promised in the writings of Moses and the prophets long ago. We are made right with God by placing our faith in Jesus Christ. And this is true for everyone who believes, no matter who we are."

And goes on to say, "For everyone has sinned; we all fall short of God's glorious standard. Yet **God, with undeserved kindness, declares that we are righteous.** He did this through Christ Jesus when he freed us from the penalty for our sins. For God presented Jesus as the sacrifice for sin. People are made right with God when they believe that Jesus sacrificed his life, shedding his blood. This sacrifice shows that God was being fair when he held back and did not punish those who sinned in times past, for he was looking ahead and including them in what he would do in this present time. God did this to demonstrate his righteousness, for he himself is fair and just, and he declares sinners to be right in his sight when they believe in Jesus" *(Romans 3:21-26 NLT)*.

In the Authorised Version of the bible, verse 26 reads like this, "To declare, I say, at this time his righteousness: that he might be *just,* and the *justifier* of him which believeth in Jesus." The writers of the Authorised chose to use the words *"just"* and *"justifier!"* which mean; to "render or declare innocent/righteous." So from this passage we can see that righteousness is not attainable through our own efforts. It has to come from God and in His economy there is nothing any of us can do to "render or declare" ourselves righteous. Thank God this is the case, because if good works were necessary, then ten million good works would never be enough!

Deception always whispers, "You don't need God!" and those who believe this are amongst those who are still convinced of their own righteousness. What they don't realise is that it's Christ's righteousness they need not their own. They certainly do "need" God!

RELIGIOUS DECEPTION IS A VERY SUBTLE

However this type of religious deception is a very subtle; the most well meaning folks still have it in the back of their minds that mere "church-attendance" weighs in somewhere in helping to make them righteous! Others believe that good deeds; like selling chicken dinners or holding fund raisers in support of God's program – helps makes them righteous! But **no kind of "fund-raiser" will even come close to procuring even the smallest of heavenly "favours" let alone any divine "contributes" towards being righteous!** Not a single work can do it!

The only solution offered us is Jesus. He is all we need! We are righteous because of Him and not independent of Him. We cannot look from afar "at" Him and think we can have what He has. **The only way we can obtain righteousness, is to be IN Christ Jesus** - because God counts the righteousness of Christ as valid - not ours! "...we are all as an unclean *thing*, and all our righteousnesses *are* as *filthy rags...*" *(Isaiah 64:6)*

Consider it like this. In the Old Testament righteousness was gained through faith. *(See Hebrews chapter 11 for the great hall of faith!)* Now in the New Testament it is no longer so. We can only gain righteousness by receiving the One who IS righteousness! Our own is filthy as said in the scripture above and this is where "holiness" comes into it. Holiness is part of righteousness; because righteousness also means "innocence." Holiness is an "innocent" lifestyle; however the only innocent one among us is Christ; blameless and pure. "Be holy because I, the LORD, am holy. I set you apart as holy" *(Leviticus 21:8 GW)*.

We are encouraged over and over again throughout scripture – in both Old and New Testaments - to stay far away from any kind of perversion... which is the exact opposite of holiness. Perversion is that which can "stain" our white *(blood washed)* robes of righteousness. We must remain spiritually "clean" once Christ has "cleansed" us, because, "Christ also loved the church, and gave himself for it; That he might sanctify and **cleanse** it with the washing of water by the word, That he might present it to himself a glorious church, **not having spot, or wrinkle,** or any such thing; but that it should be **holy and without blemish**" *(Ephesians 5:25-27)*.

Only the Holy Spirit can help do the impossible; "remain spotless, pure and blameless," in a dark world full of filth. After all God did give us His Spirit of "Holiness!"

Therefore it stands to reason that once God has declared us righteous in His sight - through Christ we have a clean slate and an "innocent" record - we cannot corrupt this again by "continuing" in sin and expecting innocent status to be "unaffected." As those who tout, "Once saved always saved," also fail to understand that it is possible to "disrobe!" In other words, we can take off our robes of righteousness anytime! We can also compromise them at any time. That's why we must "continue" in righteousness and work out our salvation with "fear and trembling" *(Philippians 2:12)*.

You can reject them *(robes)* and the blood that bought them anytime; but God's desire "that none should perish" - will never alter. He can never change, as there is no "variableness, neither shadow of turning" with Him *(James*

1:17). On the other hand "we" change all the time! Yet we must "remain" innocent.

The only way to achieve this is to "remain" IN Christ's innocence/righteousness. Only IN Christ is this possible. From start to finish and all the way through... we must keep our eyes on Christ and stay IN Him. Without Christ - we have no qualification. God the Father sees - the demons in hell see - this Righteousness of Christ in and on our lives. *(They must recognise Christ – see "Seven sons of Sceva" Acts 19:14).*

THE RIGHTEOUSNESS OF GOD REVEALED

For I am not ashamed of the gospel of Christ: for it is the power of God unto salvation to everyone that believeth; to the Jew first, and also to the Greek. For therein is the righteousness (dikaiosunē) of God revealed from faith to faith: as it is written. The just shall live by faith. For the wrath of God is revealed from heaven against all ungodliness and unrighteousness (adikia) of men, who hold the truth in unrighteousness.
(Romans 1:16-18)

In the New Testament the Greek word for **"righteousness"** used above in Romans 1:16-18 is *dikaiosunē (pronounced dik-ah-yos-oo'-nay)*, Strong's #G1343 lit. equity *(of character or act); specifically (Christian)* justification.[1]

Then the Greek word for **"unrighteousness"** also used above in Romans 1:16-18 is *adikia (pronounced ad-ee-kee'-ah)*, Strong's #G93 lit. *(legal)* injustice *(properly the quality, by implication the act);* moral wrongfulness *(of character, life or act):* - iniquity, unjust, wrong.[2]

In the Old Testament we see the Hebrew word used for "righteousness" in one of the names of God Jehovah-Tsidkenu - *yehôvâh tsidqênû (pronounced yeh-ho-vaw' tsid-kay'-noo)* Strong's #H3072 which describes this name as a symbolical epithet of the Messiah and of Jerusalem: - THE LORD OUR RIGHTEOUSNESS.[3]

Like grace, **righteousness as a gift cannot be earned; a gift is "given" and is the total prerogative of the "giver" not the receiver!** When it comes to the gift of righteousness, we must be "declared righteous" by the giver - God. When He declares us righteous, then we are righteous! Notice that righteousness was also called a "gift" in Romans 5:17, "...they which receive abundance of grace and of the **gift of righteousness** shall reign in life by one, Jesus Christ."

A gift is something that one person gives to another person, and he gives it because he wants to give it. You couldn't pay him for it. If you did, it would cease to be a gift. It would become a wage or a payment. But when a gift is given, obligation free and voluntarily, then it is a total gift. There's nothing left to do but "receive" or "reject" it!

As righteousness is such a "gift" all we must do is "receive" it. In fact - at the same moment we received Jesus Christ as our personal Lord and Saviour - right at that moment, God gave us the gift of righteousness. "Therefore, as by the offence of one judgement came upon all men to condemnation; even so by the righteousness of one the free gift came upon all men unto justification of life" *(Romans 5:18).*

The Reality of Righteousness

DECLARATION OF RIGHTEOUSNESS

The word "condemnation" means "judgement." **By the righteousness of Jesus Christ, this free gift came upon all men unto the justification or unto the declaration of righteousness.** "For just as by one man's disobedience *(failing to hear, heedlessness, and carelessness)* the many were constituted sinners, so by one Man's obedience the many will be constituted righteous *(made acceptable to God, brought into right standing with Him)*" (Romans 5:19 AMPC).

Notice, it says, "many WILL be made righteous." It did not say that, "many MIGHT be made righteousness if they work hard enough to earn it!" Just as righteousness is not something we earn neither is it something we replicate. It is purely something that God does for us. Because of Christ we are as righteous as we are ever going to get! In other words it's all because of Him. Start to finish. We can't initiate it or improve on it. It is done. When we stepped into Christ, we stepped into His righteousness. Pure and simple!

When I used to think that I had to "do" things to become righteous, I inevitably failed no matter my efforts or good intentions – as a result I felt even more unrighteous! What I failed to comprehend was that God had already declared me righteous – in Christ! God's Word is final authority on the subject; it's all about what He says, not what we say about ourselves or our feelings *(or even our denominations!)* It's easy to feel "unrighteous" at times, but that's precisely why it takes faith and not feelings to affirm the Word of God and declare; "I am the righteousness of God in Christ Jesus!" *(2 Corinthians 5:21)*

> *For if because of one man's trespass (lapse, offense) death reigned through that one, much more surely will those who receive [God's] overflowing grace (unmerited favor) and the free gift of righteousness [putting them into right standing with Himself]* ***reign as kings in life*** *through the one Man Jesus Christ (the Messiah, the Anointed One).*
> (Romans 5:17 AMPC)

What an awesome concept - **reigning in this life!** To reign is terminology normally used for kings who rule their own kingdom and this is precisely what the word "reign" literally means; to "rule." However let me point out, that we are not just meant to rule in the next life but right here in this one! REIGN IN LIFE right now today! I prefer the Amplified version of the above scripture, which says ***"shall reign as kings in life."*** In other words we are meant to rule our circumstances and everything in our immediate environment; exerting influence on all around us, just as Jesus did.

REIGNING OVER LIFE'S CIRCUMSTANCES

From the Old Testament let's use Elijah and Elisha as our example. In 2 Kings 2:8-14 we see that first Elijah and Elisha together and then Elisha alone - wanted to cross the Jordan River and there were no bridges or ferries to take them across, so verse 8 says, "Elijah took his cloak, rolled it up and struck the water with it. The water divided to the right and to the left, and the two of them crossed over on dry ground" *(NIV).* Then verse 13-14 continues with Elisha as, "He picked up the cloak that had fallen from Elijah and went back and stood on the bank of the Jordan. Then he took the cloak that had fallen from him and struck the water with it.

The Reality of Righteousness

'Where now is the LORD, the God of Elijah?' he asked. When he struck the water, it divided to the right and to the left, and he crossed over."

In closing, just imagine the scene here; he took his mantle from around his neck and slapped the water with it. Everywhere he slapped the water, dry land appeared. As the water went back, *he stepped out on that*; then he slapped another place and stepped out on that, as he walked across on dry land.

Taking dominion one step at a time! Now this is exactly what we should do over life's circumstances – taking authority one smite at a time! When we truly walk with God, we reign with Him and even the elements cannot withstand our faith in Him. *(Remember Jesus is King of kings and Lord of lords. If we reign with Him this makes us kings and lords!)*

Finally: Elijah was such a one who dared to reign in life with his God and when he prayed it didn't rain for three-and-one-half years. He **ruled** the circumstances. Jesus stopped a storm by telling the sea to be still and the waves to lie down – and they did! Then He said, **"I tell you for certain that if you have faith in me, you will do the same things that I am doing.** You will do even greater things, now that I am going back to the Father" *(John 14:12 CEV)*. Likewise as Christians, we are supposed to be the "masters" of our circumstances.

TRUTH FOR THE JOURNEY

ENDNOTES:

1. Strong, James. S.T.D., L.L.D. 1890. Strong's Exhaustive Concordance, Dictionaries (Lexicon) of the Hebrew and Greek Words
2. Ibid
3. Ibid
4. This "Truth for the Journey" has been taken from: https://watchersofthe4kings.com
5. Unless otherwise indicated, all scripture references are taken from the King James Version of the Bible.
6. Scripture references marked AMPC are taken from the Amplified® Bible (AMPC), Copyright © 1954, 1958, 1962, 1964, 1965, 1987 by The Lockman Foundation. Used by permission. www.Lockman.org
7. Scripture references marked CEV are taken from the Contemporary English Version® Copyright © 1995 American Bible Society. All rights reserved.
8. Scripture references marked GW are taken from GOD'S WORD®, © 1995 God's Word to the Nations. Used by permission of Baker Publishing Group.
9. Scripture references marked NIV are taken from the HOLY BIBLE, NEW INTERNATIONAL VERSION ®. NIV ®. Copyright © 1973, 1978, 1984 by the International Bible Society. Used by permission of Zondervan Publishing House. All rights reserved.
10. Scripture quotations marked NLT are taken from the Holy Bible, New Living Translation, copyright © 1996, 2004, 2007 by Tyndale House Foundation. Used by permission of Tyndale House Publishers, Inc., Carol Stream, Illinois 60188. All rights reserved.

Letter 7

Truth for the Journey

More than Religious Clichés

Letter to the Church, 24th September 2010

*F*or just as through the disobedience of the one man the many were made sinners, so also through the obedience of the one man the many will be made righteous.

(Romans 5:19 NIV)

For those of us who genuinely know Christ as our Lord and Saviour today, we can thank God that we have been made righteous! We can actually declare with confidence each morning in the bathroom mirror, "I am righteous!" To say otherwise would be to deny God's Word that tells us in the above scripture that *"...many shall be made righteous."*

We can of course include ourselves in that. But what does righteousness literally mean for the individual? Religious words can often stay shrouded in mystery and present tiresome clichés that never really gain any meaning in our hearts because their context is always hidden in religiosity. At one point or another many of us have found ourselves in a place where difficult words like, *"righteousness, justification, and grace,"* have been hard to master until revelation came!

In its most basic form, righteousness means "right standing with God." **It means we are "right with God"** or in other words we have a "right to stand before Him" - talking to Him as some of us would talk to our earthly fathers. I say, "...as some of us would" because not all of us have experienced a loving "relationship" with our natural fathers, if at all.

However the meaning of being made righteous, is the reality that God Himself has declared us "RIGHT with Himself," He is willing to receive us anytime and give us unlimited "access" and "proximity" to His throne of grace; a place where we are able to "enter in with all boldness" according to Hebrews 10:19. **Without any fear of rejection, judgement or eternal punishment** – because His perfect love casts out all fear. Our relationship with Him involves coming freely for "relationship and for prayer," expecting Him to grant every request that lines up with and is "according" to His Word. We are reconciled and prodigal children who have been justified, JUST AS IF WE HAD NEVER SINNED!

Some people think that being right with God means that everything we do now is RIGHT and that we are no longer capable of sin or making any mistakes at all! This of course is nonsense! On the other hand there are others who polarize by going to the opposite end of the extreme; whenever they make mistakes they convince themselves that they are no longer, "right with God" and are going to go to hell.

Let me add here, that if we can become so uncertain of our eternal future so swiftly, this is precisely why we must "know" scripture. Not informatively but by revelation. I will also suggest that "being-free" and "staying-free" are two separate phenomena. Why? **Only the truth we "know"** *(have revelation of)* **can make us free - bring constancy or security into our lives.** Only then can we stop living a yo-yo existence of – one day going to heaven – the next going to hell! "And ye shall *know* the truth, and the truth shall make you free" *(John 8:32 KJV)*.

THE TRUTH OF THE MATTER

No matter what the mistake - we are just as right with God after our mistake as we were before – why? Simply because our "right-standing-with-God" will never be "governed" by what we have done but solely upon what Christ has done. Walking away from Christ by rejecting His saving grace is something else entirely but we are talking here about "mistakes!" Wilful sin still causes disqualification - of course – but then every one of us has fallen short! "THEREFORE, [there is] now no condemnation *(no adjudging guilty of wrong)* for those who are in Christ Jesus, who live [and] walk not after the dictates of the flesh, but after the dictates of the Spirit. [John 3:18]" *(Roman 8:1 AMPC)*.

Besides our "born again" experience meant that we were "born into right standing" through Christ - as new creatures all of the old things have passed away. It is our job to remain in this "rightness" with God and enjoy it! But we must recognise that we "enjoy" such a position through Christ alone. Whereas those who are currently not "in" Christ cannot yet be considered "right-with-God" and cannot reap the benefits of such a position until they too accept Christ and what He did for them.

Even though many "good and law-abiding citizens" will fail to "enter-in" because they base their eternal future on what "they" have done and not upon what Christ has done – on their behalf. That's like still paying the bill after someone has already picked up the tab for you! Ignorance is never "bliss!" As many will sadly find out...

Therefore anyone who is not in "right-standing" with God in this way can be considered "un-righteous." **Whereas all "born-again and Spirit-filled believers" have no place doubting their salvation at all.** Having said this, if we are truly *"born-again"* then we are obligated to ACT like so! Not by way of a self-righteous attitude or pious *"holier than thou"* mentality - but a lifestyle that reflects Who we are living through and who we are walking with! *(Galatians 5:16)*

It must be added at this particular point that if the devil can get us to feel "crummy-enough" about ourselves, then he can take our effectiveness away from us. He does this by using "condemnation." People who are so easily convinced by this – must learn the difference between the "conviction" that the Holy Spirit brings and the "condemnation" that the devil brings. One demoralizes us and the other progresses us. We must remember too, that our adversary is the "master of accusation" and is meant *(by all intents and purposes)* to accuse the brethren. So why do we act so shocked when it happens!

HELP! I CAN'T GO ON LIKE THIS

His role is to "entice us into sin" and then readily "accuse us" once we yield! Nice plan... but it works every time. People the world over are living between the pendulum of temptation and condemnation. Always feeling bad about themselves - guilt ridden and demoralized. That's just the Christians!! Sad to say, but many believers have not dedicated themselves to **"renewing-their minds"** enough and such a lack of stability gives Satan all the opportunity he requires.

By the time he's done what he is meant to do – entice, tempt and accuse - we don't *feel* very righteous at all! And it's when we don't feel very righteous that we allow oppression to come upon us. We get to the point where our backs are so against the wall that we can no longer motivate ourselves; by the time it looks so bad we cry out "Help! I can't go on like this..."

What we really need to do is help ourselves! No amount of prayer or help from anyone else is going to stop this vicious cycle. **We need to be convinced of our right standing with God for ourselves - this no one else can do for us!** Either Jesus did what He did for us or He didn't. It's that precise and simple. Otherwise we will spend our whole lives analysing what we "feel" about everything – that we never really "do" anything. Exactly the devil's ploy altogether; "I must make them 'feel' so crummy about themselves so that they become so 'incapacitated, self-absorbed, insecure and ineffective' that they will pose no threat to me at all!"

It's not rocket-science! And to avoid sounding overly cynical here let me point out the critical fact that when we allow the devil to "condemn" us so much - over our individual weaknesses – to the point that we don't believe we are righteous anymore; this is when we also become convinced that God no longer hears us anymore! Then we don't even bother praying. Because we don't believe that it will work – for us! For everyone else perhaps, but not for us! *(Consequently that's another ploy of the devil – the "comparison-gap" – but oh how we don't want to get into that one!)*

All said and done – even though we like to think that we believe the bible from Genesis to Revelation; we will still be quicker to believe the devil when he starts accusing us than believe God. When we listen to his accusations, rather than taking God at His Word; what a travesty this is; especially considering all that Christ has done! Plus considering just how effective our lives "could" be if we would just remain convinced for long enough – of truth rather than the lies. "The earnest *(heartfelt, continued)* prayer of a righteous man makes tremendous power available…" *(James 5:16 AMP)*

FAITH IS NEVER BASED UPON FEELINGS!

For this reason it is paramount that we each "reach" for spiritual maturity and stop being so spiritually "insecure." The God kind of faith is never based upon feelings! Instead the bible tells us that **righteousness is a gift** from God. **Therefore we are righteous based upon FACT not upon FEELINGS and we must live according to FACT and not FEELING!** When we live in this perspective, placing facts over feelings; the feelings eventually catch up!

Nevertheless the Christian who swings from pillar to post, between feeling and fact is usually insecure. Only the secure Christian is dedicated to living according to FACT before FEELING. They develop the kind of lifestyle that is conducive with "obedience and willingness" as mentioned in Isaiah 1:19 – **their feelings following but never lead!**

In closing let me emphasise the balance. God created feelings and emotions. Therefore without a doubt they have their place. For example we are not austere robots, but creatures able to express love, happiness and joy. This was God's design. However, it was never God's design for us to BASE our faith upon them. When we put so much stock in our "feelings" we always end up misled, into a place of disobedience.

Our feelings were never designed to lead but to follow. This is how we "enjoy" an experience. We first have the experience and then the feelings are supposed to follow. That's how we know whether we enjoyed it or not! First thing first; the chicken or the egg! We must always remember that faith follows fact never feeling. But feelings don't become obsolete. **They just follow - and help "complete" the experience rather than create it!**

Personally I live my life this way. I base my faith on the facts of God's Word; that I AM righteous and nothing can change that as long as I remain in Christ. My emotions cannot manipulate any of the facts. I just accept the fact and put my faith in it and rejoice that even though I am not worthy - the choice was His and not mine. He chose me anyway! I accept His "divine" decision every day and live with the fact that God counts me righteous. Hallelujah!

ENDNOTES:

1. This "Truth for the Journey" has been taken from: https://watchersofthe4kings.com

2. Scripture quotations marked AMP are taken from the Amplified® Bible, Copyright © 2015 by The Lockman Foundation. Used by permission. (www.Lockman.org)

3. Scripture references marked AMPC are taken from the Amplified® Bible (AMPC), Copyright © 1954, 1958, 1962, 1964, 1965, 1987 by The Lockman Foundation. Used by permission. www.Lockman.org

4. Scripture references marked KJV are taken from the King James Version of the Bible.

5. Scripture references marked NIV are taken from the HOLY BIBLE, NEW INTERNATIONAL VERSION ®. NIV ®. Copyright © 1973, 1978, 1984 by the International Bible Society. Used by permission of Zondervan Publishing House. All rights reserved.

Letter 8

Truth for the Journey

Winning in Life through a Winning Mind

Letter to the Church, 15th June 2010

For as he thinketh in his heart, so is he...
(Proverbs 23:7 KJV)

I love to see people succeed in life, just like the artist treasures his painting and the craftsman his violin, so our Creator cherishes His design! He is concerned about our dreams, goals and our ability to be happy and to enjoy life. But all said and done, none of us can truly enjoy life unless we STAY IN OUR RIGHT MINDS!

Success is being happy. Happiness is basically feeling good about our lives and our plans. Two forces are vital to happiness: our relationships and our achievements. The

Gospel also has two forces: the Person of Jesus Christ, and the principles He taught. One is the Son of God; the other is the system of God. One is the life of God; the other is the law of God. One is the King; the other is the Kingdom. One is an experience with God; the other is the expertise of God. One is heart-related the other is mind-related. Salvation is experienced *"instantaneously"* while God's wisdom principles are learned *"progressively,"* and both are essential for success and happiness.

In everything therefore we must make it a priority to protect our thought lives. Some folks like to shout about their "double portion" but have never dealt with their fanatic in the attic! In reality the same Holy Spirit will make us deal with this chief opponent *first.* There is no uncertainty about it, we must conquer our minds! This is a place where there can be no demilitarized zone, no middle ground. Either it belongs to the enemy or to God.

When it comes to the mind there is no grey fudge. It is black or white, all or nothing. Another thing is for certain; where there is no discipline there is no Holy Spirit! He is never chaos. He is always order! Anyone who is successful today *(whether secular or Christian)* is someone who has mastered their minds with sheer "discipline." From business men to politicians, sports personnel or record breakers; they set their "minds" on a goal and don't deviate.

INCAPACITATED WITH MENTAL DISTRACTIONS

Sadly in retrospect many Christians are incapacitated *(out of action!)* because they have never learnt how to protect their thought lives. Satan bombards them with fear, hatred, suspicion depression, mistrust and a host of other mental distractions *(or should I say "disorders?!")* But why does this "zone" have to be the most vulnerable area of our lives? Because happiness really does begin between our ears! **The mind is the drawing room for tomorrow's successes or failures; what happens there** *(in our minds)* **happens in time.**

As scripture clearly tells us *"...as he thinketh in his heart, so is he" (Proverbs 23:7 KJV)*. So what you *"keep in mind"* from day to day is really what is shaping your future - positive or negative! Making *"mind-management"* a MUST for any believer who seeks to be an over-comer! In fact it's not hard to recognise an over-comer from an defeatist; simply someone who is self adjusting vs. someone who lives in perpetual internal chaos and confusion! And their outer world usually shows it too!

Conquering or mastering the mind can be called "renewing" the mind, which is why Paul wrote to the Romans saying,

> *Do not conform any longer to the pattern of this world, but be transformed by the renewing of your mind. Then you will be able to test and approve what God's will is - his good, pleasing and perfect will.*
>
> *(Romans 12:2 NIV)*

Our mind must be renewed. God's salvation includes the mind. The late Dr. Bob Gordon said, "The mind is an actual battlefield in the experience of many people. Lack of mental discipline leads to chaos in the thought life, an inability to discern truth from error and bondage to an imagination that is able to breed negative ideas and dreams."[1]

THE BATTLEFIELD IS IN THE MIND

In her bestseller, **"The Battlefield of the Mind"** Joyce Meyer also states that there is a war going on where our minds are the battlefield, the good news being that God is fighting on our side! In her book Joyce uncovers the tactics of the enemy and gives a clear-cut plan to triumph in the fight for your mind. She teaches how to renew the mind through **the Word and stand victoriously in the battlefield of the mind.** Our enemy uses a deliberately devised plan of deceit and lies. Attacking our minds with doubting thoughts, fear and paranoia to erode our resistance; investing any amount of time in order to defeat us.[2]

However the Word of God has the power to cleanse our minds regardless and it is all important that we read and meditate on His Word and remain obedient to it. We must read, meditate and speak the Word continually, taking captive every thought to make it obedient to Christ (2 Corinthians 10:5). *"Do not let this book of the law depart from your mouth; meditate on it day and night, so that you may be careful to do everything written in it. Then you will be prosperous and successful" (Joshua 1:8 NIV).*

WEAKNESSES OF OUR NATURAL MIND

- It is hostile to God *(Romans 8:5-7)* unbelievers are often "hostile" towards the gospel.

- The things of God are foolish to the natural mind: *(1 Corinthians 2:12-14)*
- The natural mind is blinded to God by Satan: *(2 Corinthians 4:4)*
- The natural mind is the source of violent and evil desires: *(Ephesians 2:3)*
- The natural mind is futile in its thinking and darkened in its understanding: *(Ephesians 4:17-18)*

Perhaps you can imagine how Joshua might have felt after he had just successfully crossed over the Jordan River through an awesome act of faith, which took him and all the people across only to arrive in Jericho *(Joshua 6:1-f)* to look up and see **"those gigantic walls"** that surrounded that great City. As a military man his mind must have gone to work strategizing, "Well if we build some ramps, we'll come at it like this... we can make a hole and maybe get through..." But instead of attacking the walls, God's instructions were to **"march"** around it in silence for seven long and probably hot days - surely this sounded so foolish to Joshua's naturally military mind?!

Joshua was as natural as you or I and it would have been as much of a discipline for him as it is for us, to learn to stop thinking in his natural mind, and be disciplined enough to flow with the mind of God, especially when the instructions seemed so completely "un-natural" and out of sync with his natural instincts! And as a military figure Joshua had to lay his own strategy down in order to accept the Lord's.

This is not always easy. But then submission rarely is! It's based on trust, faith and relationship AND dying to self!

But as we know on the seventh day when they all marched around in obedience seven times "shouting and praising" the Lord, it was then and only then - out of sheer obedience and discipline - that the walls came tumbling down. Let's be honest, **it takes a disciplined mind just to keep our mouths quiet!** "For out of the abundance *(overflow)* of the heart, his mouth speaks!" *(Luke 6:45 NKJV; emphasis added)*

Finally remember this - faith is not chatty or spontaneous - it is too deliberate! And disciplining our minds has to be a determined - on purpose - and deliberate act of our faith. Only this will get the job done, no matter how long it takes. Then and only then can we truly say that we have conquered our own minds and now have "the mind of Christ" *(1 Corinthians 2:16)*.

ENDNOTES:

1. "Understanding the Way" by Bob Gordon, Copyright © 1987. Published by Marshall and Scott, London, United Kingdom

2. "Battlefield of the Mind" by Joyce Meyer, Copyright © 1995. Published by Harrison House, Inc. Printed in USA

3. This "Truth for the Journey" has been taken from: https://watchersofthe4kings.com

4. Scripture references marked KJV are taken from the King James Version of the Bible.

5. Scripture references marked NIV are taken from the HOLY BIBLE, NEW INTERNATIONAL VERSION ®. NIV ®. Copyright © 1973, 1978, 1984 by the International Bible Society. Used by permission of Zondervan Publishing House. All rights reserved.

6. Scripture references marked NKJV are taken from the New King James Version. Copyright © 1982 by Thomas Nelson, 1982 by Thomas Nelson, Inc. Used by permission. All rights reserved.

LETTER 9

Truth for the Journey

Signs of a Renewed Mind

Letter to the Church, 18th June 2010

*C**asting down imaginations, and every high thing that exalteth itself against the knowledge of God, and bringing into captivity every thought to the obedience of Christ...*

(2 Corinthians 10:4-5)

Let's give you some examples from scripture of what a "renewed mind" looks like!

1. Our spiritual understanding is increased: *(Ephesians 1:18).*
2. Our minds become the vehicle of the Holy Spirit and His gifts, discernment and revelation.

3. We have a changed life through understanding Truth, where we take the cleansing power of God's Word to sanctify our minds and set us free from wrong thoughts. Paul in Ephesians told us to put off the old self, which is being corrupted by its deceitful desires, to be made new in the attitude of our minds; and to put on the "new" self, created to be like God in true righteousness and holiness *(see Ephesians 4:22-24; Hebrews 4:12).*

I remember Ian Andrews once saying, that when he began to minister in the early 70's, he was told to "go and preach the gospel" but by the time he had stuttered out the words "g o o d   m o r n i n g" it was already *afternoon!* Ian prayed *"Lord heal me of my stutter and 'then' I will go and preach the gospel for You."*

Nonetheless people were still going to Ian with all kinds of stuttering problems and were getting healed *left-right-and-centre,* which made it even more frustrating for him. However through that process God taught Ian Andrews how to rely totally on the Holy Spirit and not upon his own understanding, strengths, circumstances or facts *(a good lesson for all of us!)* Yet Ian had suffered with a *severe* stammer for most of his life and would say to God, *"Lord I'd be thrilled to preach the gospel and pray for the sick - only heal me first."*

But God had the last word on the subject and would say to him, "No! *You go as you are, then everyone will know who the Healer is, that it is Me - I will heal you gradually - AS YOU GO"* and that is precisely what happened! God did it! "AS HE WENT - IN OBEDIENCE!"

For Ian, it was a humbling and sometimes frustrating experience and yet he found that yielding to God was the only way forward. And to his surprise, God's life began to flow through him as people got healed and most importantly it did not ever depend on "Ian" or how he "felt." Pure and simple - when the people heard that Jesus took their pains and sicknesses upon Himself, they looked to "God" and were healed.

STEPS FOR THE JOURNEY

Our greatest need right now as Christians is the "Holy Spirit" - He is the only one who can help us understand the profoundness of all of these things. He alone can show us just how to go about renewing our minds.

These few steps are part of the process:

1. **First we must "completely" surrender our minds to the Lord:** *(Romans 12:1).* Complete means complete! This is not a weight watchers plan that we join for a few weeks till normal life takes over - NO! This is God we are talking about - and what He does in our lives is for KEEPS. The idea is this, we give Him our minds and He gives us the Mind of Christ. It's more than a fair deal I would say!!! In fact it is a pure act of grace.

2. **Then we must submit all of our "thinking" to the Cross:** *(2 Corinthians 10:5)*

3. **We must make continual and deliberate choices where to place of our minds:** *(Colossians 3:2)*

4. **And examine and test the content of our thought lives:** Whatever comes IN we must test: is this of God or Satan? Is it Carnal - is it flesh? *(Philippians 4:6-7)*

5. **We must immediately refuse every thought that is wrong or sinful:** In God's Word it says that we should think of things that are honest and true, the devil says we should think of things that are dishonest and untrue *(Philippians 4:8-9).*

6. **We must commit to think God's Thoughts:** When a situation comes up, we must not deal with it by human reasoning. Why? Even Jesus explained to His disciples that He must go to Jerusalem and suffer many things, even unto death, but Peter rebuked Him saying; "Never, Lord! This shall never happen to you!" And Jesus turned to him and said, "Get behind Me, Satan! You are a stumbling block to me; you do not have in mind the things of God, but the things of men" *(Matthew 16:21-23 NIV).*

   Consider this... just momentarily. Ponder on what He said, "...you have not IN MIND the things of God but the things of men." Now this is not hard to understand, it's not rocket science! What we have in MIND is absolutely everything. Therefore for the serious Christian we better mind the things of God and not the things of this world.

7. **It is not enough to think about something that needs our decision or prayer:** We must think about it the way God thinks about it. God's thoughts went

beyond the suffering that Jesus would encounter in Jerusalem, beyond the rejection, humiliation, the cross and the grave. In fact God's thoughts looked forward to the resurrection; the triumphant Ascension, the outpouring of the Holy Spirit, to Christ's glorious Second Coming, and ultimately towards His reign upon this earth.

8. **Read and meditate on the Word:** "Do not let this book of the law depart from your mouth; meditate on it day and night, so that you may be careful to do everything written in it. Then you will be prosperous and successful" *(Joshua 1:8 NIV).*

9. **Create a Climate of confidence in every circumstance:** We must speak about our EXPECTATIONS of SUCCESS, not our EXPERIENCES or FAILURES. "Death and life are in the power of the tongue..." *(Proverbs 18:21)* We must rehearse previous achievements in our minds and remember that our "sufficiency is of God..." "In whom we have BOLDNESS and access with CONFIDENCE by the faith of him" *(Ephesians 3:11; see also 2 Corinthians 3:5).* Our position of superiority over circumstances was established when we became children of God *(Romans 8:16, 17, 37).*

10. **Help Others Become Successful:** Assist others in discovering their gifts, talents and dreams. You will reap what you sow. The motto of the WAY OF THE WINNER is, "What you make happen for others, God will make happen for you." When Job prayed

for his friends, his captivity was turned *(Job 42:10)*. When the poor widow gave to the prophet, God gave to her *(1 Kings 17)*. "Knowing that whatsoever good thing any man doeth, the same shall be receive of the Lord" *(Ephesians 6:8)*.

11. **Value the God-Connection:** Recognize God as a plus factor. He is NEVER a DISADVANTAGE to us, ALWAYS an ASSET. He wants us to succeed and He "hath pleasure in the prosperity of His servant" *(Psalms 35:27)*. Read scriptures on a daily schedule. Practice the power of prayer. Make Jesus Christ Lord of your life. "Acquaint now thyself with him, and be at peace: thereby good shall come unto thee" *(Job 22:21)*. "...as long as he sought the Lord, God made him to prosper" *(2 Chronicles 26:5)*. **Finally we can say that life only changes when our daily priorities change.**

12. "Finally,... brothers, whatever is true, whatever is noble, whatever is right, whatever is pure, whatever is lovely, whatever is admirable - if anything is excellent or praiseworthy - think about such things. Whatever you have learned or received or heard from me, or seen in me - put it into practice. And the God of peace will be with you" *(Philippians 4:8-9 NIV)*.

Mike Murdock once said; "Winners are simply ex-losers who got mad. Winning doesn't start around you it begins INSIDE you. SO MAKE UP YOUR MIND!" Be Informed, we must secure all pertinent information concerning our goals. "Wise men layup knowledge..." *(Proverbs 10:14)* "My people are destroyed for lack of knowledge..." *(Hosea 4:6)* Observe. Read. Maintain an "information file." Utilize the expertise of others. "He that walketh with wise men shall be wise..." *(Proverbs 13:20)*

ENDNOTES:

1. "365 Wisdom Keys" by Mike Murdock, Copyright © 2012. Published by Wisdom International Inc. Printed in the USA

2. This "Truth for the Journey" has been taken from: https://watchersofthe4kings.com

3. Unless otherwise indicated, all scripture references are taken from the King James Version of the Bible.

4. Scripture references marked NIV are taken from the HOLY BIBLE, NEW INTERNATIONAL VERSION ®. NIV ®. Copyright © 1973, 1978, 1984 by the International Bible Society. Used by permission of Zondervan Publishing House. All rights reserved.

Letter 10

Truth for the Journey

Our God Given Antidote to Stress

Letter to the Church, 23rd March 2010

*B*ut the fruit of the Spirit is love, joy, peace, longsuffering, gentleness, goodness, faith, Meekness, temperance: against such there is no law.

(Galatians 5:22-23 KJV)

Today I was on my instant messenger and up popped an advert with a slim fast product *(a fat burning pill that promised results in just one week!)* with the usual clever marketing, various tributes and a doctor to legitimize the product..! Admittedly it was all very tempting to believe; nonetheless all *"short cuts"* make me dubious. Why? Because they usually don't work long term! Even something as important as salvation you can't jump the fence! *(Luke 13:24)*

As far as weight loss is concerned only the right kind of lifestyle that beats stress can also conquer the waist line! As experts say that the liver produces fat when under stress; *(stress is such a successful tool for the devil because once he can get us to engage with stress; we self destruct!)* proving the point that no amount of expensive creams, pills or other products can change us outwardly when the change we need is inward. Even *scientifically proven* products are a waste if we are stressed out all the time. Stress will still increase those signs of aging no matter how much you spend on that cream! **And while every effort *should* be made to improve our lives; without proper inward adjustments, all outward adjustments are sure to be counter-productive!**

QUALITY OF LIFE *IS* IMPORTANT

But this all opens up a deeper topic for me; the feel good factor and everybody trying to be the next *"feel good guru!"* Quality of life *is* important and that sense of genuine *well-being...* After all we *are* meant to live life more abundantly and it *is* the *good news* that we are advocating and not the bad! But consider how thin the line is, that exists between the feel good factor and compromising the gospel altogether!

If global persecution towards Christianity hit tomorrow, will we be amongst those who "love not their lives unto death" *(see Revelation 12:11)* or will we side with the popular notion; *"well this just does not make me feeeeel good; if I'm not happy doing it then I am just not going to do it..!"* How far will we take this feel good gospel without undermining the whole plan of salvation?

Every soldier who signs up has the opportunity to die, can he enjoy life in-between!? That's the question! What's more you don't have to be molested as a child to be stressed out as an adult *(forgive the stark analogy...)* in fact the average person today is stressed out and we all have different reasons for being so! Whole congregations today admit to being stressed out. **It's an epidemic!** But as Christians we should never be stressed out, once again, stress is a successful tool for the devil.

In reality he needs to do very little while we do the rest. Little effort... big results..! Practically the entire body of Christ live under stress making us unproductive for Christ and ineffective in our witness.

What remedies this current paradox better for the Christian other than the *fruits of the spirit? (see Galatians 5:22)* **Our best antidote is to seek first the Kingdom of God, which is "...*righteousness, peace and joy in the Holy Spirit*"** *(see Matthew 6:33, Romans 14:17).* Basically, **stress free living is the result of living by the Spirit** "...against such there is no law" *(see Galatians 5:23 KJV).* His burden is light and His yoke is easy and His joy is our strength... *(see Matthew 11:30; Nehemiah 8:10)*

Are we confused with inspirational speaking versus preaching? It is true that while we *must* encourage people to live life to the fullest and be happy, we must not *sell-out or compromise* the gospel in the process! And while precious people this world-over are dying for the sake of the gospel, there are others who just want to *"feel good"* about it! *Do we really want to be that shallow?*

Why be a Christian if we can't overcome in life? However God's provision of the fruits enable us to walk in this life empowered by his Holy Spirit, and with His divine nature. We are not meant to succumb to the pressures of this world. ***God gave us his Holy Spirit to empower us, to do more than just speaking in tongues!***

ENDNOTES:

1. This "Truth for the Journey" has been taken from: https://watchersofthe4kings.com
2. Scripture quotations marked KJV are taken from the King James Version of the Bible.

Letter 11

Truth for the Journey

Are You Free or Just Out of Control?

Letter to the Church, 26th March 2010

*R**ebellion is as sinful as witchcraft and stubbornness as bad as worshiping idols. So because you have rejected the command of the Lord, he has rejected you...*

(1 Samuel 15:23 NLT)

Have you ever considered why cancer is such a threat in today's world? Why are so many people suffering with this unsolvable problem? With today's technology the way that it is, cancer still seems to defy even the best minds. What is the cause, what is the cure? Listening to **Dr Don Colbert** and **Brother Kenneth Copeland** discussing this subject I heard the simplest definition for cancer that I've heard yet... basically cancer is the result of, **"...cells rebelling against the body!"** It is all a result of rebellion, manifesting in the body at cell level, rogue cells attacking the body like a bunch of lawless thugs... breaking down the body's immune system.

There can be several reasons for this; unhealthy living and unhealthy attitudes. **Sowing seeds of rebellion over time will produce a harvest.** It's one thing that we can be certain of..! We must be watchful over the type of seeds that we sow...

> *That is why many of you are weak and sick and some have even died. But if we would examine ourselves, we would not be judged by God in this way. Yet when we are judged by the Lord, we are being disciplined so that we will not be condemned along with the world.*
> *(1 Corinthians 11:30-32 NLT see also AMP)*

However not all sick people, whether from cancer or otherwise, are guilty of rebellion! We must be careful not to adopt condemning theologies. I had a certain friend some years ago who was very dear to my wife and I... but I found out the hard way one day what his theology truly consisted of. I spent five hours reeling with pain while passing gall stones from my bladder... perhaps it was the nearest experience to giving birth for a male! I was rushed to an Italian hospital late at night, to have my kidneys scanned and to be seen by specialists... but when I spoke with my dear friend by phone to ask for prayer, besides other harsh opinions he mainly implied, "maybe you are in sin?!?!" That day I discovered what Job must have felt like!

O' boy, I was truly shocked and it occurred to me then, that people only lose that kind of harsh theology when they themselves are sick! On the other hand sin *can* be a factor in sickness but not *always* and we must safeguard ourselves from adopting theologies that are either "all inclusive and compromising" or "condemning and judgmental." They are equally as bad!

FIVE LONG HOURS BEGGING GOD

If you have ever passed gall stones then you'll know just how painful that was for me! I was literally on my knees for five long hours begging God; like all of us do, when in a fix we can't control! You bet the first thing I did was check my heart! *(But in the end it just turned out to be, too many years of drinking too much strong English tea and drinking too little water! I've changed my lifestyle a little since then!)*

There are all kinds of reasons for thinking the way that we do... many times our own experiences dictate to us... and if we are hard on ourselves, then we are likely to be hard on others too. My friend was less than understanding and sadly his theology was very condemning.

So having been on the receiving end of that, I certainly don't want to dish out any condemnation upon the sick... but having said that, **there has to be real weight to the Word of God. If everything can be just explained away, then it has little value to it.** Cancer is spiritual but eventually manifests itself in the flesh. Even our churches suffer from spiritual rebellion, cancers... in fact I dare say that the Body of Christ is riddled with it! Metaphorically speaking...!

So many people have no respect for authority or even godly order... whether in secular life or in Christendom. They walk out of jobs the minute they don't like something or file out of churches the minute they don't agree! This amounts to a cultural blend of rebellion. And as a result a harvest of rebellion is being reaped upon entire generations of people. People are afraid of cancer mainly because they can't control it... but neither can you control a rebellious heart...

We have to make sure that we are not stubborn and rebellious; the harvest on that type of seed is not the type of harvest we want!

> *The human heart is the most deceitful of all things, and desperately wicked. Who really knows how bad it is? But I, the LORD, search all hearts and examine secret motives. I give all people their due rewards, according to what their actions deserve.*
> *(Jeremiah 17:9-10 NLT)*

There is order in the body as God created it... but cancerous cells rebel against that order... wreaking havoc in the body, breaking it down. And a house that is divided against itself eventually falls... Being rebellious is synonymous with wanting our own way - rather than, "not my will Father but yours..." Instead we want to be in control of our own lives... yet the harvest from that will be just as hard to control! In fact most people, who claim to be free, are actually OUT OF CONTROL!

Are You Free or Just Out of Control?

ENDNOTES:

1. This "Truth for the Journey" has been taken from: https://watchersofthe4kings.com

2. Scripture quotations marked AMP are taken from the Amplified® Bible, Copyright © 2015 by The Lockman Foundation. Used by permission. (www.Lockman.org)

3. Scripture quotations marked NLT are taken from the Holy Bible, New Living Translation, copyright © 1996, 2004, 2007 by Tyndale House Foundation. Used by permission of Tyndale House Publishers, Inc., Carol Stream, Illinois 60188. All rights reserved.

Letter 12

Truth for the Journey

We Need to Act

Letter to the Church, 16th March 2010

For everyone born of God overcomes the world. This is the victory that has overcome the world, even our faith.

(1 John 5:4)

Brother Hagin often used to say, *"...we need to act like we believe it!"* Act free; not bound again to slavery. **Satan knows whether you know - your legal rights or not - by the way you live your life and the words you speak!** If we act like we don't believe it - Satan knows that probably we don't! Those who have been justified act justified. They are no longer under the sentence of death but have been acquitted and found not guilty.

Note: The prosecution has no more defence against us - no more argument. IF and again I say IF we are in Christ. Why? Because, "Therefore, there is now no condemnation for those who are in Christ Jesus" *(Romans 8:1)*. Only Faith in TRUTH - in the Superseding Spiritual Fact - will move God to answer your Prayer and Move Satan to Flee from you as he should.

The just shall live by faith. This is our legal way to live - by faith! Which includes the fruits of the spirit - against which there is no law? Everything about this life has spiritual reality, whether atheists choose to believe that or not, it remains fact. And it is all about legalities. What's lawful and what's not etc... And we as Christians need to know that and not live a life of continual ignorance; for God plainly stated that, *"...we perish for the lack of knowledge" (Hosea 4:6 KJV)*. Even though He called the foolish things to confound the wise - He didn't expect those foolish things to stay foolish!! On the contrary we are ever encouraged to have the eyes of our understanding opened and to gain the spirit of wisdom and revelation *(Ephesians 1:17, Proverbs 4)*.

Precisely, we are not called to a life of perpetual ignorance but a life of revelation - as true disciples - accountable to truth and living it out as it's revealed. The term "Progressive Revelation" refers to the fact that by grace we are endlessly permitted to **"learn obedience"** and grow in our faith - as the young Christ did in his earlier years *(Hebrews 5:8)*. We too have to "grow up" spiritually - which requires us growing from *"faith to faith, glory to glory"* *(2 Corinthians 3:18; Romans 1:17)*. It's a process of learning, growing, changing and correction - a time of much needed grace for our ignorant and somewhat innocent mistakes! *(Psalms 44:26)*

PROSECUTION OR DEFENCE

Satan as said before is a legalist. Like the best smartest lawyer or prosecution available to *"oppose"* the saints as in Zechariah 3:1; see also Revelation 12:10 *(NKJV)*,

> *...the **accuser of our brethren, who accused them before our God day and night,** has been cast down. And they overcame him by the blood of the lamb and by the word of their testimony, and they did not love their lives to the death.*

Some say that since the time of the book of Job *(considered one if not the oldest books of the bible - but not in chronological order)* Satan has not been able to oppose the saints directly in the presence of the Lord, like we see in Zechariah 3:1 and other - but we see here in the New Testament, Revelations 12:10, the word **accused** is used in the "PAST TENSE." So one may want to conclude that he is no longer allowed to accuse us day and night in the direct presence of God perhaps *(throne room)* but we do know for sure that he could for a season of time.

However notice in the same chapter verse 17 *(NKJV)* it says, **Satan is not after the "Convert" - He's after the "Disciple!"**

> *...and the dragon was enraged... and he went to make war with the rest of her offspring, **who keep the commandments of God and have the testimony of Jesus Christ.***

To continue the theme of the court room further - let's consider the fact that the Amplified Bible calls him an **"evil genius"** *(John 16:11 AMPC)*. It helps to know what you're up against...!

You need not to be ignorant of your opponent *(2 Corinthians 2:11)*. **Satan is not ignorant of the facts!** Just imagine in a court of law - if one day the "prosecution" or "defence" in a high profile case decided to violate the court, the law or the Judge, only in a wild attempt to prove their case! **Their means would only serve to disqualify their end!** *(They would be thrown out of court even if all their evidence were true!)* A court of law MUST be taken seriously and MUST only be based upon the proven or otherwise disproved FACT; but never on emotional blackmail or feelings. Someone can only be acquitted or put away *"on the grounds of reasonable evidence."*

SATAN IS STILL AN ACCUSER

Whether directly or indirectly Satan is still an ACCUSER *(Revelation 12:10)*; in fact we can see clearly that he no longer stands in the direct presence of God to accuse us anymore - the conflict is far more direct, *"...he went to make war..."* (NKJV) Remembering that he was thrown out of the presence of God *"...has been cast down"* verse 10. <u>Down</u> where? To the earth; *"Woe to the inhabitants of the earth and the sea! For the devil has come down to you, having great wrath, because he knows that he has a short time"* (verse 12).

Jesus' combat with Satan in the wilderness was face to face! Word to word... (Mark 1:13) And the wrestling of Ephesians 6 involves direct contact, "Put on the full

We Need to Act

*armour of God so that <u>**you** can take **your** stand against the devil's schemes...</u>" (verse 11)*

<u>*...they overcame him by the blood of the Lamb and by the word of their testimony...*</u>
(Revelation 12:11)

As Derek Prince once said, *"this was **direct**, (not in-direct) conflict..."*[1] mentioned there in Revelations 12:11 but also in Ephesians 6:12 where it tells us what we don't wrestle with *(flesh and blood)* before it goes on to confirm that our direct conflict is with ranking powers of darkness..!

For WE DO NOT WRESTLE against flesh and blood, <u>BUT</u> against principalities, against powers, against the rulers of the darkness of this age, against spiritual hosts of wickedness in the heavenly places.
(Ephesians 6:12 NKJV)

The Master Accuser: It's safe to say, that one must not assume to go after an experienced accuser and try and beat him at his own game! Taking *("railing")* accusations to an "accuser" is like taking coal to fire!! *(We must overcome evil with good, Romans 12:21).* One accuser to another creates a common ground. If Michael had attempted to achieve his aims outside of his *(delegated/authorised)* boundaries, he would have usurped his own authority - thus usurping the Lord.

THE SUPERSEDING SPIRITUAL FACT

There is not meant to be any common ground between light and dark, truth or lie. So we come against Satan as Jesus did - with TRUTH the superseding spiritual FACT.

A dear saint who had been gloriously healed of breast cancer, shared of her struggle, and in her testimony she made this statement, *"all my petitions, all my crying, failed to move God to compassion or Satan to flee! In fact none of my self pity, not any one of my emotions, my piety, nor even my virginity or holy living could move HEAVEN OR HELL - EXCEPT MY FAITH!"*

She found out – only through living it out - that the ONLY SUBSTANCE ABLE TO MOVE HEAVEN or HELL - WAS HER FAITH! God is not moved by many words *(Matthew 6:7-8)* or favouritism - works - just by FAITH. That's why only faith pleases Him because He knows that it's the only way we can obtain His blessings made available to us through Christ *(Matthew 21:21, 1 John 5:4)*.

Only Faith in TRUTH - in the superseding spiritual fact - will move God to answer your prayer and move Satan to flee from you as he should. Faith comes by hearing and hearing by the word of God. Jesus only used truth - He did not accuse Satan. He used His only weapon - TRUTH.

There is no truth or love in Satan, like there is no light in darkness. There was no common ground, because Jesus was using the truth, with the truth in His heart *(rightly divided 2 Timothy 2:15)*. Whereas Satan was misusing the truth, in order to deceive. The motive was not the same. Jesus used the truth, not just to save or gratify self, but to save others.

We Need to Act

ENDNOTES:

1. "The Blood of the Lamb" by Derek Prince, online article, Publication Date 2011, https://www.derekprince.com/teaching/11-3

2. This "Truth for the Journey" has been taken from: https://watchersofthe4kings.com

3. Unless otherwise indicated, all scripture references are taken from the HOLY BIBLE, NEW INTERNATIONAL VERSION ®. NIV ®. Copyright © 1973, 1978, 1984 by the International Bible Society. Used by permission of Zondervan Publishing House. All rights reserved.

4. Scripture references marked AMPC are taken from the Amplified® Bible (AMPC), Copyright © 1954, 1958, 1962, 1964, 1965, 1987 by The Lockman Foundation. Used by permission. www.Lockman.org

5. Scripture references marked KJV are taken from the King James Version of the Bible.

6. Scripture references marked NKJV are taken from the New King James Version. Copyright © 1982 by Thomas Nelson, 1982 by Thomas Nelson, Inc. Used by permission. All rights reserved.

Letter 13

Truth for the Journey

Faith to Live By

Letter to the Church, 30th July 2010

The person who has God's approval will live by faith. But if he turns back, I will not be pleased with him. We don't belong with those who turn back and are destroyed. Instead, we belong with those who have faith and are saved.

(Hebrews 10:38-39 GW)

In Galatians 2:20 Paul the Apostle said, *"I live by the faith of the Son of God..."* as so we must. It's worth noting and considering that just as Jesus provided all things for us to overcome He also provided us with HIS OWN FAITH! Now that's a thought! We have Christ's faith. No longer do we have to think that we have "little faith" as He often told His disciples. I guess compared to His faith, ours is puny!

"Is not all faith the same?" You may ask, but the answer to that question is simply "No!" Sure every human being has the ability to operate in "natural" faith but not everyone can operate in "supernatural" faith. Take for instance business men or mere sports champions who all realize their goals and achievements via their "natural faith" but obviously not, "by the faith of the Son of God!" Therefore, it can be said without any doubt that both NATURAL and SUPERNATURAL FAITH co-exist. However without Christ we are restricted to operating in "natural" faith alone.

Having separated and defined both types of faith it must be said that a lot has been achieved through "natural" faith alone and those who have dared to operate in this natural faith have been some of the world's greatest achievers! And still they have not known Christ. So although limited this natural faith evidently packs a punch regardless! When people exercise faith in anything *(being totally convinced)*, then it's hard to shake them off, discourage them or dampen their spirit.

A SIGNIFICANT DIFFERENCE

The significant difference between the two is that "all-things-natural" are also wholly "temporal" and for this reason it would be correct to say, **"Futile is every effort that starts and ends in the flesh"** because they are entirely restricted to the natural realm. That which is spiritual however can transcend and operate in any realm; giving **"all-things-spiritual"** a clear advantage over those things that can only operate within the one realm!

To accomplish spiritual goals therefore, such as our chief commission given to us by Christ *(see Mark 16:15-18)* simply nothing other than "supernatural faith" will suffice, in fact we need what Paul had, the very *"...faith of the Son of God!"*

Once again, on several occasions Jesus told certain individuals *"Oh ye of little faith..!"* *(see Matthew 6:30; 8:26; 16:8; Luke 12:28)* This was not a mere criticism but an actual "FACT." Why? Because Jesus Himself knew that our "natural" faith was puny in comparison to His and wholly inadequate in achieving heaven's mandate! Personally I believe that Jesus was purposefully and continually provoking His disciples to rely on HIS FAITH rather than their own. Once we master this, we too can echo Paul and have *"...the God kind of Faith"* mentioned in Mark 11:22 and Galatians 2:20!

If there be doubt left about the need to separate faith from "natural" to the "supernatural" 1 Corinthians 2:4 says *"...your faith should not stand in the wisdom of men, but in the power of God."* Once we achieve this we can truly become the "history makers" of our generation.

Smith Wigglesworth once said, *"Only believe! God will not fail you, Beloved. It is impossible for God to fail. Believe Him. Rest in Him, for God's rest is an undisturbed place where heaven bends to meet you. God will fulfil the promises made to you in His word - believe it!"*[1]

TRUST COUPLED WITH SUPERNATURAL FAITH

While looking into the dynamics of faith, we could hardly bypass the subject of "trust." Faith can't exist without it, in fact they are synonymous *(indelible, intrinsic elements of the same thing!)* Which of us can have faith in a God we can't trust? Even so, there are elements of faith that go way *beyond* mere "trust" *(even if "trust" is part of faith's central core).*

In the Old Testament certain scriptures use faith in conjunction with trust; found in such scriptures bearing the Hebrew words *châsâh* and *bâṭach;* generally taken to mean: *have confidence in, trust, make refuge.* For example Psalms 36:7 "How excellent is thy loving kindness, O God therefore the children of men put their trust *(châsâh)* under the shadow of thy wings." Also in Proverbs 3:5 "Trust *(bâṭach)* in the Lord with all thine heart; and lean not unto thine own understanding."

The entire list of "heroes of faith" found in the eleventh chapter of the book of Hebrews *(to whom New Testament believers look for inspiration)* were made up of individuals who simply put their TRUST in God! As God "partnered" with them, He added His "supernatural" element to their trust! All faith is a gift.

However in the New Testament faith is considered both a supernatural "gift" and a "fruit." Yes anything "given" by God is technically a "gift" but we are talking in context with the supernatural "gift" of faith *(an endowment)* and then the "fruit" of the spirit *(of character)* as mentioned in 1 Corinthians 12:9 & Galatians 5:22; the significant between them simply being "power" and "lifestyle!" One works supernaturally, the other is "outworked" in our personality by the Holy Spirit.

Faith to Live By

In his book, **"Faith to Live By"** the late Derek Prince wrote, "Fruit then, expresses character. When all nine forms of spiritual fruit are present and fully developed, they represent the totality of Christian character, perfectly rounded off, each form of fruit satisfying a specific need and each complementing the rest. Within this totality, the fruit of faith may be viewed from two aspects, corresponding to two different, but related, uses of the Greek word pistis. The first is trust; the second is trustworthiness."[2]

There we have it! Trust coupled with supernatural faith vs. trustworthiness coupled with character. I prefer to say that faith is actually "supernatural trust" on a level that the natural is incapable of. And trustworthiness is part of the "divine nature" that must be outworked in our lives; as we are naturally incapable of being trustworthy in character without the Holy Spirit!

"Now the just shall live by faith *(pistis):* but if any man drawback, my soul shall have no pleasure in him" *(Hebrews 10:38).* This word *pistis (pis'-tis)* is the Greek word used for FAITH in Hebrews 10:38 and Romans 10:17 - which helps take things to another level!

This is where "faith" goes from being simple "trust" *(or confidence)* to actually focusing on "getting the job done" or "achieving the goal!" This little Greek word πίστις *(pistis)* is taken primarily to mean: *persuasion, moral conviction (especially reliance upon Christ for salvation); assurance, belief and fidelity.* "Without *pistis* it is impossible to please God." *(Hebrews 11:6)* Although it did not say "without trust it's impossible to please God" pistis could literally be translated as the "the ultimate level of TRUST."

Nevertheless just as *rhēma and logos* are "partners-inseparable" the same is true of faith and trust; yet whether we discuss supernatural or natural elements of faith and trust our dependability rests on God. Without Him we achieve nothing sustainable. In partnership with Him our lives can be limitless!

ENDNOTES:

1. "Smith Wigglesworth Only Believe: Experience God's Miracles Every Day." Copyright © 1998, Published by Whitaker House, Printed in the United States of America

2. "Faith to Live By" by Derek Prince, Copyright © 1977, Published by Whitaker House, Printed in the United States of America

3. This "Truth for the Journey" has been taken from: https://watchersofthe4kings.com

4. Unless otherwise indicated, all scripture references are taken from the King James Version of the Bible.

5. Scripture references marked GW are taken from GOD'S WORD®, © 1995 God's Word to the Nations. Used by permission of Baker Publishing Group.

Letter 14

Truth for the Journey

Marginalizing Faith is Not Pro-Active

Letter to the Church, 7th September 2010

Be honest in your evaluation of yourselves, measuring yourselves by the faith God has given us.
(Romans 12:3 NLT)

As we have discovered in history it only serves us well when we take stock of the truths gained throughout the ages. As we glimpse into times past particularly during the Church's brief history we can easily conclude that a general type of faith is by no means equal to the challenges that present themselves! We can discuss faith in very general terms by saying that ALL faith is supernatural and ALL faith is a gift from God.

Although faith as we know it has very specific elements, it has not been my endeavour in this particular Truth for the Journey to discuss the ins and outs of faith and all its particulars. Rather, my focus here is resting upon the realities of "living" by faith. Just the very word "living" poses the fact that it's something we must do "everyday" - not dissimilar to breathing! In fact in order for us to "live- by-faith" effectively - it then must be as consistent as our breathing! Consider that!

Main-stream or "nominal-Christianity" would suggest that faith is something we just step "into" only when necessary or when a miracle is required. They focus on different "strengths" of faith opposed to looking at faith in terms of something we are meant to "live-by." **God never gave us our faith-equipment simply for "occasions and events" but for "life!"** We must allow faith to have the priority it deserves in "everyday-life" or should I say "life-style?" And as our title above suggests; marginalizing faith is simply not pro-active, because we should never "trivialize" faith - ever!

Where the Old Testament told us that men would live by their "own" faith *(Habakkuk 2:4)*, Paul in the New Testament spoke of living not by his own faith but by the faith of the Son of God *(Galatians 2:20)*. So in the New Testament things changed a little where faith was concerned *(except where the New quotes the Old!)* Therefore it's vital that we have a "revelation" about this, that no longer does a great and arduous "onus" rest on our shoulders but rests on Christ! Simply because "our" faith is "feeble-stuff" and lacks terribly! Jesus recognized this in his own disciples, whom He referred to on more than one occasion as having "little faith," sometimes asking them, "Where is your faith?" *(Luke 8:25; Matthew 14:31; 16:8).*

This was not a compliment that Jesus was paying them and we can argue about the "size" of faith - like when Jesus spoke in Matthew 17:20 about faith being as a mustard seed. But I will suggest to you that He was explaining - in natural terms - to natural men - who were still at that time limited in their understanding - about something that was supernatural. He was helping them to see that even when they try to "measure" the "God kind of faith" with natural limitations; it will still achieve mighty exploits because the God kind of faith is "limitless!"

Those who walk with God today have been given this kind of faith *(the faith of God or the God kind of faith - as seen in Mark 11:22-24)*, which is given us by His Spirit, as it tells us in Romans 12:3, "...according as God hath dealt to every man the measure of faith..." and in 1 Corinthians 12:9 "...faith by the same Spirit."

When the Lord Himself ever gives something to us - we can be sure that it is totally complete - *(not broken or missing anything)* this includes the faith that He measured to us. I do not want to wade too deep into *vague* waters here by over generalizing a huge subject such as this, but I am intrigued by the lack of concept that many Christians have concerning the fact that they are meant to *LIVE* by faith.

If we just focus on the word *LIVING* we can safely conclude that our everyday experience should testify of our continual walking and living by the Holy Spirit and the Word;

showcasing that our experience of God is a LIVING reality - not mere isolated incidences; opposed to a daily WALK. This is **NOT** LIVING BY FAITH but occasional experiences of faith only; usually brought on by necessity or emotion!

DARE WE TAKE THE CREDIT!

More to the point; we were neither designed nor hard-wired to do any exploits for God in our "own" strength much less live by our "own" faith. Likewise living out the fruits of the Spirit is not a test of our agility or spiritual prowess - dare we take the credit?!

"God wants yielded vessels and not golden ones..." was the time famous adage from the much loved Kathryn Kuhlman. How well she knew that no amount of *(personal)* talent could adequately prepare or equip her for the task God had placed in front of her. Therefore **she chose a posture of perpetual preparedness - a lifestyle of unrelenting yieldedness and surrender!** "I am crucified with Christ: nevertheless I live; yet not I, but Christ liveth in me: and the life which I now live in the flesh I live by THE FAITH OF THE SON OF GOD, who loved me, and gave himself for me" *(Galatians 2:20).*

ALL things pertaining to life have been bestowed on us - including the faith of the son of God. Not any old faith but specifically *HIS* faith. Scripture could not have been more specific! Would He really have gone to such lengths to give us His own blood yet spare us His faith...? I am convinced not!

Marginalizing Faith is Not Pro-Active

FAITH IS A CHOICE

We can choose to live by our own faith if we want to, in textbook fashion *(I call this textbook Christianity!)*, but **treating the bible like a technical manual only produces impersonal robots!** However we know this thing is much more a *LIVING PRACTICE* than it ever was a *THEORY* only to be studied or agreed with! Sadly many Christians only ever offer "mental-assent" to their bibles; rather than stepping into its pages and allowing it to become a LIVING reality! Far be it that we just commit our lives to well told stories..!

So then, all considering history's widest portals the greatest achievements were made by those who chose to allow faith to come upon them not just for the sake of occasion but chose to live by an unrelenting faith *(for decades)* securing victories and breakthroughs we still celebrate to this day.

True is the fact that even in his own strength, man has been able to achieve magnitudes! The tower of Babel is a testimony to that fact. As created beings we are able to co-create and with various levels of intelligence we have proven unquestionably ingenious! Nevertheless we have divine commission upon us and only a supernatural faith is capable of achieving this. I would like to go even further and suggest that no matter how collectively talented we may be; ONLY THE "FAITH OF THE SON OF GOD" CAN PERFORM THE VERY "WORKS OF GOD!"

According to faith teachers, the gift of faith defined in 1 Corinthians chapter twelve "...*comes upon us only at specific times for specific purposes, as a supernatural gift from God to receive miracles."* Dare I revise the point that ALL faith is supernatural and ALL faith is a gift from God? Not only did Paul tell us to live by the faith of God but also Mark 11:22 told us to have the **GOD KIND OF FAITH.**

The specifics of faith vary of course and are much broader than discussed here, along with the fact that the "GIFT" of faith as discussed by the many Faith preachers does "lift..." I still maintain that we must LIVE by the faith of the Son of God **DAILY** *(after all is it any less supernatural or prepared?),* with immersed lifestyle; not just for occasions!

Jesus' faith was not just for "effect or occasion" either. It was not a three year road-show! Instead Jesus was ready IN SEASON AND OUT, "God anointed Jesus of Nazareth with the Holy Ghost and with power: who went about doing good, and healing all that were oppressed of the devil; for God was with him" *(Acts 10:38).*

I will finish by concluding that although we live in this world, we are certainly not possessed by it! As finite beings **we have been given the right to operate successfully in both realms; the supernatural and the natural. However it is clear that only the GOD KIND OF FAITH can facilitate our success in "both."**

Our success in the Kingdom of God is measured primarily by our OBEDIENCE *(Isaiah 1:19; Matthew 6:33)* nevertheless any "success" that we might enjoy within the boundary of our heavenly commission *(Mark 16:15-18)* can only be legitimate when **LIVED OUT BY THE FAITH OF THE SON OF GOD.** Then the credit is *all HIS!* So let us live synonymous with

Paul's timeless statement; "...the life which I now live in the flesh I live by the faith of the Son of God" *(Galatians 2:20).*

ENDNOTES:

1. This "Truth for the Journey" has been taken from: https://watchersofthe4kings.com

2. Unless otherwise indicated, all scripture references are taken from the King James Version of the Bible.

3. Scripture quotations marked NLT are taken from the Holy Bible, New Living Translation, copyright © 1996, 2004, 2007 by Tyndale House Foundation. Used by permission of Tyndale House Publishers, Inc., Carol Stream, Illinois 60188. All rights reserved.

Letter 15

Truth for the Journey

His Faith Alone Can Accomplish

Letter to the Church, 12th March 2010

B<i>y the faith OF the Son of God.</i>
(Galatians 2:20)

I remember some years ago within the early years of my ministry, a time when I was seeking the Lord to use me. Earnestly praying and seeking God's face; like many young men I really wanted to do everything that God had called me to do. I loved hearing stories of the saints of old who down through the ages etched their mark on history as we know it. I have always been inspired to read about their small beginnings and how God took them from nothing and made a something out of them!

Smith Wigglesworth was such a man, simple in speech, unsophisticated; a true man's-man, whom I could relate to. Regardless of education or eloquence, he was potent for the Lord! These types were my inspiration and I remember one day, crying out to God, *"If only, I could be like Smith Wigglesworth."* To which I remember God's reply as if it were only yesterday, *"Why limit yourself?"* At first not understanding I soon realised what He was communicating, *"Don't be bound by another man's achievements."* Be sure to, *"Take your eyes off of men and get them back on Me."*

God never requires us to clone ourselves nor strive to fulfil another man's destiny. In fact it's **only as we keep our eyes on Him to hear His guiding voice, will we possess faith sufficient enough to fulfil our own divine destiny - without LIMIT!**

Long ago I realised this simple but life changing truth; superseding all my best efforts! Ample is faith all the time we yield our lives to THE FAITH OF THE SON OF GOD. Trying to muster faith is pitiful! No! "I live," Paul said in Galatians 2:20, "by the faith OF the Son of God."

> *I am crucified with Christ: nevertheless I live; yet not I, but* **Christ liveth in me:** *and the life which I now live in the flesh* **I** *live by* **"the faith of the Son"** *of God, who loved me, and gave himself for me.*
> *(Galatians 2:20)*

Through yielding we not only have sufficient faith "IN" but also enjoy the faith "OF" the Son of God. **It is His faith in us alone that can accomplish the destiny which He has set**

before us! "And I am convinced and sure of this very thing, that He Who began a good work in you will continue until the day of Jesus Christ [right up to the time of His return], developing [that good work] and perfecting and bringing it to full completion in you" *(Philippians 1:6 AMPC)*.

My prayer for you, precious reader is that you not only study to show yourself approved, but that you earnestly look to God for the path which He has set before you. Yielding to His faith that never stops reaching for your DESTINY! My heart aches whenever I think of all the wasted potential in the world today. Staggering millions of people! With talents untapped, underdeveloped and un-applaud.

DON'T LIVE BELOW YOUR POTENTIAL

Others choose to live far below their potential and talents in the spirit of fear and procrastination. Listen, no one appreciates an educated fool! Nor the expert who knows EVERYTHING about SOMETHING but NOTHING ELSE! People don't much care for the "educated guess" either! What cuts the ICE is our ability to hear God and live out those instructions.

> *He who is able to hear, let him listen to and give heed to what the Spirit says to the assemblies (churches). To him who overcomes (is victorious), I will grant to eat [of the fruit] of the tree of life, which is in the paradise of God.*
> *(Revelation 2:7 AMPC)*

In the last 26 years of walking with the Lord *(at the time of writing)* I have seen much success simply by obeying HIS

VOICE. This does not negate knowing His written Word of course! Nevertheless RELATIONSHIP without Rhema is a misnomer or an oxymoron!

In the process of time, I have also seen many go through systems of education, with great earnest, endeavour and expectation only to come out the other side fully equipped with qualifications they never use! Many fail to step beyond the preparation and allow God to USE them to the max.

Our intelligence and education surrounding the Word of God must never cease to be paramount, but one must never substitute obedience for knowledge alone. Yet the process of equipping us with skill in the things of God is only to aid our obedience to His voice. Rightly dividing His Word in the spirit of revelation has its purpose buried in the fact that we aught to live obediently to the now Word of God; living revelation!

My encouragement for anyone studying with earnest in preparation for what they believe God has said to them is this. In all your pursuit of knowledge, never fail to develop a hearing ear! And in the hearing, is the doing...! Sadly a relatively small percentage of all students ever end up doing what they actually studied for. My prayer is that you not only fulfil your potential and purpose but WALK it through to completion in all obedience.

The Apostle Paul said, "For we are his workmanship, created in Christ Jesus unto good works, which God hath before ordained that we should walk in them" *(Ephesians 2:10)*.

It's evident that God assigned a special path in life for you. It is your duty to find out what that path is and walk it through, with the Faith of the Son of God.

ENDNOTES:

1. This "Truth for the Journey" has been taken from: https://watchersofthe4kings.com
2. Unless otherwise indicated, all scripture references are taken from the King James Version of the Bible.
3. Scripture references marked AMPC are taken from the Amplified® Bible (AMPC), Copyright © 1954, 1958, 1962, 1964, 1965, 1987 by The Lockman Foundation. Used by permission. www.Lockman.org.

Letter 16

Truth for the Journey

Faith Operates by Believing and Saying

Letter to the Church, 9th March 2010

*O*ut *of the abundance of the heart the mouth speaketh…*

(Matthew 12:34-35)

This is not theory. It is fact. Charles Capps says, "It is spiritual law" and "it works every time it is applied correctly." SO IT IS A SPIRITUAL LAW THAT GOD NEVER DOES ANYTHING WITHOUT S-A-Y-I-N-G IT FIRST. He is a faith God who releases His faith in His Words. *"And Jesus answering saith unto them, Have faith in God"* (Mark 11:22). A more literal translation of the above verse says, *"Have the God kind of faith"* or *"the faith of God."*

Ephesians 5:1 literally tells us to be imitators of God as children imitate their parents. To imitate God, you must talk like Him and act like Him. He would not ask you to do something you are not capable of doing. Jesus Himself operated in the faith principles of Mark 11:23, and Matthew 17:20 while He was on earth. He spoke to the wind and sea. He spoke to demons. He spoke to the fig tree. He even spoke to dead men! They obeyed His SPOKEN WORDS... which had power and influence.

He operated in the God kind of faith; God is a faith God. And most importantly, because God released HIS faith through Words; we must follow suit. Our words are usually loaded with fear or faith, life or death *(see Genesis 1:3)*.

Jesus was imitating His Father and getting the same results! In John 14:12 Jesus said, *"He that believeth on me the works that I do shall he do also; and greater..."* These principles of faith are based on spiritual laws which work for whosoever applies them and sets them in motion. Do we really want all the negative things we have been confessing to come to pass? Do we really believe for those things to happen? Of course not! But if Jesus came to us personally and said, "From this day forward it will come to pass, that every thing that you say will happen exactly as you say it;" it would change our vocabulary for ever!

Spoken words program our spirit *(heart)* either towards success or defeat. Words are truly containers; carrying and producing whatever they contain; *"...faith cometh by hearing and hearing by the Word of God"* (Romans 10:17). Faith comes more quickly when we hear ourselves quoting, speaking, and saying the same things God says. We will more readily receive God's Word into our spirits by hearing ourselves speaking it... than if we hear someone else speaking it.

Much of what the Father supplies to the body of Christ is furnished through our confession. This is not simply our positive, premeditated confession expressed in prayer; it consists of everything that comes out of our mouths. *"But I tell you, on the day of judgment men will have to give account for every idle (inoperative, nonworking) word they speak"* (Matthew 12:36 AMPC).

The International Standard Bible Encyclopedia *(ISBE)* states that the Greek word *(argós)* generally used for *"idle or idleness"* in the New Testament literally meant: inactive, useless, empty gossip, nonsensical talk.[1] Whereas the Strong's Concordance #G692 takes argos *(pronounced ar-gos')* as generally meaning: inactive, unemployed; lazy, useless; barren, idle or slow.[2]

Our words are the overflow and the revelation of our heart condition! Christ, as the *"High Priest of our confession"* (Hebrews 3:1 NKJV), takes our words, whether in faith or unbelief, and allocates back to us eternal life in proportion to our words. When our tongue is unbridled, James tells us that our negative confession *"...sets on fire the course of our life, and is set on fire by Hell"* (see James 3:6).

In Hebrews 3:1 we are instructed to *"...consider the Apostle and High Priest of our profession, Christ Jesus."* The word translated as profession in that verse can also be translated as confession. God appointed and anointed Jesus to be High Priest over our confessions or our words of faith.

HE IS RESPONSIBLE FOR BRINGING OUR WORDS TO PASS

1 Corinthians 1:4-5 also tells us that Jesus enriches our utterance. That is, He takes our words of faith and enriches them with His Anointing. So no matter how we look at it, the words we speak carry the very creative force of Almighty God behind them. They WILL come to pass!

God created us to be the Prophets of our own lives! Our destinies are within our reach - within our very mouths! It's our words - not anyone else's - which determine our success or failure in life *(Romans 10:8-9)*. Our words either bring good things into our lives or they bring evil things *(Matthew 12:34-37)*. Throughout the New Testament we find teaching on four basic kinds of confessions.

The First Confession found in the New Testament is the confession of sin taught by John the Baptist and Jesus to the Jewish people in their day. This act of confession however, is not what we know today as Christian repentance. Actually, the confession of sin and water baptism that we read about in Matthew 3 and Luke 3 was an act by the people of Israel under the Abrahamic *(or Old)* Covenant. Prior to Jesus going to the cross, the Jews knew what it was to confess their sins and repent, but their sins were only "covered" in atonement by the blood of an animal which was sacrificed once a year. It wasn't until the sacrifice of Jesus' blood that sin could actually be wiped out and not just covered up *(see Hebrews 10)*.

The Second Confession is described in the New Testament and applies to everyone; the confession of a sinner.

Faith Operates by Believing and Saying

It's what we now know as the prayer of salvation. In John 16, when Jesus told His disciples about the soon coming Holy Spirit, He explained that the Spirit would come to convict *"the world"* of sin. But what were these *"sinners"* to do, once convicted by the Spirit? Basically, the confession of a sinner under the New Covenant is simply, "JESUS IS LORD."

> *The word is nigh thee, even in thy mouth, and in thy heart: that is, the word of faith, which we preach; that if thou shalt confess with thy mouth the Lord Jesus, and shalt believe in thine heart that God hath raised Him from the dead, thou shalt be saved.*
> *(Romans 10:8-9)*

Third Confession, today the Church is full of Christians who have no idea how to confess their sins once they do step out of fellowship with the Father - which is our third New Testament confession. The bible says, if you have sin in your life, get it out - confess it, repent of it, get rid of it. Once you do, stand on 1 John 1:9, which says, **"If we confess our sins, he is faithful and just to forgive us our sins, and to cleanse us from all unrighteousness."**

According to 1 John 1 and 2 when we are out of fellowship with the Father, when we sin - we know it. That's the time to get rid of it. Immediately! After all, 1 John 2:1 assures us that, **"If any man sin, we have an advocate with the Father, Jesus Christ the righteous."** Don't run from Him when you sin, Run to Him. The moment we confessed our sin, is the moment we got rid of it. By faith, we spewed it out of our mouths and God was faithful and just to forgive us and cleanse us.

The Fourth Confession found in the New Testament is the confession of our faith in God's Word, our faith in Christ - or His Anointing - our faith in God the Father, and our faith in the faithfulness of Jesus as our High Priest. We must remember whatever we receive from God, we receive it by CONFESSION. Our mouths are our own *"Master Key to Life!"* Again the apostle Paul wrote to the Hebrews: *"...consider the Apostle and High Priest of our confession Christ Jesus"* (Hebrews 3:1 NKJV).

To take a closer look, the word "confession" in the Greek actually means, *"Saying the same thing as; saying what God says."* It's an affirmation of a bible truth we are particularly embracing, *(or)* repeating with our lips, the thing God has said in His Word, which we believe with our heart. You might say, if you are mindful of the natural, you will live in the world, but if you are mindful of the Lord, you will live by Faith.

WHAT YOU FEED YOU BREED

"From the Fruit of his lips a man enjoys good things, but the unfaithful have a craving for violence. He who guards his lips guards his life, but he who speaks rashly will come to ruin" *(Proverbs 13:2-3 NIV)*. Our confessions - the words we constantly speak day after day - determine what we receive from God, whether it's salvation, physical healing, peace or financial prosperity.

What's more, for the rest of our eternal existence, this principle of faith working hand in hand with our confession will never change. Jesus told His disciples in Mark 11:22; *"Have faith in God,"* or, as one translation puts it, *"Have the faith of God" (YLT).* In verse 23, He went on to explain how that faith process works.

> *Whosoever shall say unto this mountain, be thou removed, and be thou cast into the sea; and shall not doubt in his heart, but shall believe that those things which he saith shall come to pass; he shall have whatsoever he saith.*
> *(Mark 11:23)*

Faith operates by believing and saying and saying and saying. It is our confession or words of faith that bring possession. We see this in Romans 10:10, *"With the heart man believeth... and with the mouth confession is made..."* And in Matthew 12:34-35, *"Out of the abundance of the heart the mouth speaketh..."*

We lay hold of the word by receiving it by faith, and then CONFESSING it. The same process which got us saved and the very process by which we receive all else God has promised. Remember, once we lay hold of the promises of God with our faith and our confession, that's when Jesus' enriching Anointing and ministry come into play. That's why the Apostle Paul told Timothy that, *"Words of faith"* nourish, but idle words starve the spirit and make it weak (see 1 Timothy 4:6-7). So let's do what Hebrews 10:23 says – Let's, *"Hold fast the profession of our faith..."* It is our CONFESSION of faith, after all, that makes the difference to life or death.

Three Steps to Take:

1. Ask According to His Word.
2. Act on Faith in His Word.
3. Praise Him in Response to His Word.

ENDNOTES:

1. Orr, James. M.A., D.D., General Editor, ISBE - International Standard Bible Encyclopedia; e-Sword ® version 7.6.1 Copyright © 2000-2005. All Rights Reserved. Registered trade mark of Rick Meyers. Equipping Ministries Foundation. USA www.e-sword.net.

2. Strong, James. S.T.D., L.L.D. 1890. Strong's Exhaustive Concordance, Dictionaries (Lexicon) of the Hebrew and Greek Words

3. This "Truth for the Journey" has been taken from: https://watchersofthe4kings.com

4. Unless otherwise indicated, all scripture references are taken from the King James Version of the Bible.

5. Scripture references marked AMPC are taken from the Amplified® Bible (AMPC), Copyright © 1954, 1958, 1962, 1964, 1965, 1987 by The Lockman Foundation. Used by permission. www.Lockman.org

6. Scripture references marked NIV are taken from the HOLY BIBLE, NEW INTERNATIONAL VERSION ®. NIV ®. Copyright © 1973, 1978, 1984 by the International Bible Society. Used by permission of Zondervan Publishing House. All rights reserved.

7. Scripture quotations marked NKJV are taken from the New King James Version®. Copyright © 1982 by Thomas Nelson, Inc. Used by permission. All rights reserved.

8. Scripture quotations marked YLT are taken from the Young's Literal Translation of the bible.

Letter 17

Truth for the Journey

The Perils of Double Mindedness, Doubt and Unbelief

Letter to the Church, 17th August 2010

A person who has doubts shouldn't expect to receive anything from the Lord. A person who has doubts is thinking about two different things at the same time and can't make up his mind about anything.

(James 1:7-8 GW)

Let us first look at double mindedness; which is designed to stop us receiving from God and in fact is synonymous with being double-spirited. If you look up this word "double-minded" in the Authorized Version of the bible *(KJV)* and use the Strong's Concordance[1] or the Vine's dictionary[2] to discover its original Greek meaning you will find that "double-minded" (δίψυχος *dipsychos*) actually means **"two-spirited!"**

Now this adds a whole new emphasis on being double minded?! In other words we cannot successfully live in two different kingdoms or operate in *(by)* two different spirits at the same time *(i.e. the spirit of this world & the spirit of God / the kingdom of God & the kingdom of darkness)* it just does not function! *(See Strong's #G1374).*[3]

In fact being double minded and doubting is practically the same thing, so when we step into doubt, we step into instability as verse eight tells that a double minded person is "...unstable in all of his ways" *(James 1:8)*. Doubt literally means *to waver in judgement; to hesitate in indecision and to distrust.* Most Christians find themselves - at some point - in this sad condition and then wonder why they are **spiritually and emotionally "confused!"**

For example, when asked, most Christians would say that they believe what the Word says about a situation but also admit that they always have a *"Plan B" (contingency arrangement!)* just in case it doesn't quite work out as God said it would! **That's like going forwards only to go backwards!** James 1:6-8 says; "...let him ask in faith, nothing wavering. For he that wavereth is like a wave of the sea driven with the wind and tossed. For **let not that man think that he shall receive anything of the Lord."**

UNBELIEF OR DOUBLE MINDEDNESS

Now unbelief is different to double mindedness or doubt in that it won't even "consider" plan A; instead it just "deserts" God altogether as seen here in Hebrews 3:12 "...brethren, take care, lest there be in any one of you a wicked, unbelieving heart [which refuses to cleave to, trust in, and rely on Him], leading you to turn away and desert... the living God" *(AMPC)*.

This scripture clearly warns against the unbelieving heart that "refuses to... trust." In fact from the very onset "unbelief" is decidedly ***negative, unreasonable and faithless;*** where doubters are a little more subtle in their contemplation; *"I believe God's Word; it's just not working for me!"* Unbelief on the other hand, has no intention of flowing with God.

In fact, unbelief cannot be accused of being "double-minded" at all; with its flat refusal to believe! It is simply "hostile" to God; again Hebrews above warns of the "wickedness" of the unbelieving heart but here in Romans 8:6 it talks of the sheer "hostility" of the carnal mind towards God, "Now the mind of the flesh [which is sense and reason without the Holy Spirit] is death [death that comprises all the miseries arising from sin, both here and hereafter]. But the mind of the [Holy] Spirit is life and [soul] peace [both now and forever]. [That is] because the mind of the flesh [with its carnal thoughts and purposes] is hostile to God, for it does not submit itself to God's Law; indeed it cannot" *(Romans 8:6-7 AMPC)*.

In other words doubt "wavers" between making decisions, where unbelief has already decided! "How long halt ye between two opinions? if the LORD be God, follow him: but if Baal, then follow him. And the people answered him not a word" *(1 Kings 18:21)*.

So there you have it, pure and simple; unbelief is a satanic force and is unambiguous *(clear-cut)* in its approach. It holds itself to a "complete-denial" of deity and refusal of truth. For instance there is always someone who will say, *"I believe that speaking in tongues is of the devil."* This in itself is "refusing" God's Word not "doubting" it. There are many people in unbelief today simply because they do not believe the verity of God's Word.

We even have theologians who teach that angels do not exist while in the New Testament Jesus Himself told of how the angels came to feed and minister to Him, and in the Old Testament for instance - Psalm 91 - it is unquestionably talking about angels! So although clearly present in His Word they still deny it!

Then there are those who say there is no devil. Well then I can only say that Jesus must have been hallucinating or imagined some weird and wonderful happenings out there in the desert! However the Word clearly says that the devil tempted Jesus in the wilderness; in fact Jesus Himself told us that we would cast out devils in His name *(Mark 16:17-18)*.

It is sad to say that those who consider themselves to be *"believers"* are the ones who often suffer from unbelief the most! In fact in Africa *(where I have travelled extensively)*, Europe is known as the "dark continent" which has churches full of "unbelieving believers!?" What a parody *(distortion)* and a poor legacy that we have left the rest of the world! In fact it's a spiritual travesty!

ENDNOTES:

1. Strong, James. S.T.D., L.L.D. 1890. Strong's Exhaustive Concordance, Dictionaries (Lexicon) of the Hebrew and Greek Words

2. Vine's Expository Dictionary of New Testament Words, by W.E. VINE, Printed by Lowe & Brydone Printers Ltd, Thetford, Norfolk

3. Strong's Exhaustive Concordance (Ibid)

4. This "Truth for the Journey" has been taken from: https://watchersofthe4kings.com

5. Unless otherwise indicated, all scripture references are taken from the King James Version of the Bible.

6. Scripture references marked AMPC are taken from the Amplified® Bible (AMPC), Copyright © 1954, 1958, 1962, 1964, 1965, 1987 by The Lockman Foundation. Used by permission. www.Lockman.org

7. Scripture references marked GW are taken from GOD'S WORD®, © 1995 God's Word to the Nations. Used by permission of Baker Publishing Group.

Letter 18

Truth for the Journey

The Perils of Fear

Letter to the Church, 17th August 2010

He that overcometh shall inherit all things; and I will be his God, and he shall be my son. But the fearful, and unbelieving, and the abominable, and murderers, and whoremongers, and sorcerers, and idolaters, and all liars, shall have their part in the lake which burneth with fire and brimstone: which is the second death.

(Revelation 21:7-8)

In the previous Truth for the Journey we looked at the subjects of "double-mindedness, doubt and unbelief" but now we must look at the participation that fear plays. As revealed in our opening scripture above, fear and unbelief work very closely together, if not hand in hand! In actual fact it's also worth noting that "fear and unbelief" take "first place" on the list of who will end up in the lake of fire!

As mentioned in the scripture above, the word used for "fear" in the original Greek (δειλός *deilos*) comes from a root word *deos* meaning to **"dread"** or to be **"timid"** and implies **"unfaithfulness"** *(see Strong's #G1169)*. Interestingly the word used for "unbelieving" - in the original Greek *(compound word)* primarily means **"faithless, passive and untrustworthy"** *(see ap'-is-tos #G571 & #G4103 where pistos [belief] becomes a-pistos! The addition of an "a" in front of pistos [belief] brings it into the negative form - just as adding "un" to belief makes it un-belief!)*[1]

Now there are those who reckon that there is such a thing in the bible as "the-law-of-first-mention." This is debatable of course, but if we were to take this literally, that would make the positioning of "fear" *(principally)* and "unbelief" *(successively)* - on this doom list in Revelations - somewhat more interesting! Especially considering whose company they share - such as the "abominable *(repulsive and detestable)* and murderers, idolaters and liars..." what a nasty list they top! It must be that God Himself finds them so offensive that they come out first on the hit list!

Other translations prefer to use the words "cowardly and unfaithful" instead of "fearful and unbelieving," but either way they seem to be of major "offense" to God.

Gratefully those of us who are in Christ do not suffer with fear. We know that in 2 Timothy 1:6-8 it says, **"God**

didn't give us a cowardly *(fearful)* **spirit** but a spirit of power, love, and good judgment. So never be ashamed to tell others about our Lord..." *(GW; emphasis added)* In addition from the Old Testament Isaiah declared, **"Fear not [there is nothing to fear], for I am with you;** do not look around you in terror and be dismayed, for I am your God. I will strengthen and harden you to difficulties, yes, I will help you; yes, I will hold you up and retain you with My [victorious] right hand of rightness and justice" *(Isaiah 41:10 AMPC)*.

FEAR IS FAITH IN REVERSE GEAR

Now let's look more closely at the characteristics of fear. Firstly it would be correct to say that **"fear is faith in reverse-gear!"** Think about it for a moment. If faith is the "substance" of good things desired. Fear is also the "substance" of bad things not desired. Again if you turn to the Greek #G5287 in the Strong's you will discover that "substance" used here in Hebrews 11:1 also means "concrete essence!"[2]

This would allow verse one to be read like this; "Faith brings the *concrete essence* of things *expected* and the *proof* of things not seen!" Reverse this equation and it could read like this instead; "fear *(or faith in reverse)* brings the *concrete essence* of things *expected* and the *proof* of things not seen!" This is confirmed by what Jesus told the centurion, "...go thy way; and as thou hast believed, so be it done unto thee" *(Matthew 8:13)*.

Admittedly there are times when "believing" is the last thing we "feel" like doing especially in a crisis, but that's when we must understand that **faith is not an emotion it**

is a decision! In fact, generally speaking if we wait for our emotions to motivate us - we would never do anything significant for God! *(Emotions fail where faith is always robust!)*

In fact fear is actually putting our faith in what the devil can do rather than what God can do. Having said that fear and faith are not on "equal-par" *(faith is far greater)* and perhaps this is why fear is so offensive to God? However the chief reason that any of us fear something is because we are really "convinced" that it will come to pass. That's what worry is all about. If we didn't believe it could come to pass - then there would be no reason to worry!

Worry in itself is counter-productive and energy zapping, because it cannot "stop" anything, it is "passive" and can only "dwell" on the negatives *(or the problem)* instead of the "solution" which **only helps "draw" the trouble closer!** Job is the classic example of this truth. **"For the thing which I greatly fear comes upon me, and that of which I am afraid befalls me.** I was not or am not at ease, nor had I or have I rest, nor was I or am I quiet, yet trouble came and still comes [upon me]" *(Job 3:25-26 AMPC).*

Job "practiced" his fear continually and as a result - his fear was "great" in strength. Although by way of conflict the scriptures declare that Job dwelt in safety, we see this in the accusation Satan brought against God, *"You've hedged him about on every side, and I can't get to him"* (see Job 1:6-12). Satan's sly request was then for God to "strike" everything that Job had, in order to disprove his faith.

Now I personally believe that God did not just "grant" this request out-right but actually replied with a statement of fact instead. See in verse 12 how God said to Satan; *"He IS in your power."* In other words, "he is ALREADY in your power!" It is important therefore to realize here that God did NOT put Job in that position rather Job put himself there. He found himself in Satan's grasp simply because of the continual "fear-rituals" he engaged in for his children *(see Job 1:5)*. This very fear contributed to dissembling of his protective "hedge" and all that he had *(verse 10)*. **Remember if we lose our position *(of faith)* we always lose our possession!**

FEAR AND FAITH ACT LIKE MAGNETS

Fear therefore gives Satan just the opportunity he is looking for. And yes! He is LOOKING. *"Be sober, be vigilant; because your adversary the devil, as a roaring lion, walketh about, seeking whom he may devour..." (1 Peter 5:8-9)* Inevitably fear always puts us in an unfavourable position. Where faith lifts us, fear pulls us down. This type of fear that takes us where we don't want to go is simply named "DREAD" and is very effective indeed. When we "dread" something long enough, we end up doing or saying the exact things we have dreaded and end up in precisely the position we didn't want to be in! Remember Job. His fear came upon him. Both fear and faith act like magnets - drawing good things or bad towards us. So watch out!

Dread is "forward" looking, just like faith is, but entirely in the negative realm and it uses our "imaginations" to help build mind-pictures of those things that we are dreading. This is exactly the same way that faith operates. Where we must "see" ourselves - by faith - doing or obtaining the very thing we are reaching for. The prerequisite *(condition)* is that we must "see" it before we possess it - naturally. Like the youth who sees himself driving "long" before he even goes to driving school! This is faith in operation in simple terms! Or Father Abraham who was required to "see" himself as the father of many nations before he actually was!

However "dread" will make us see *(and persistently see)* the very things that we don't want to happen, *(dread is synonymous with trepidation, nervousness and anxiety)*. If we yield and think about dreadful things long enough or dwell on them hard enough, then they will eventually be drawn our way! As said previously - this is literally "faith in reverse" and something we must not engage in.

More importantly it is "mounting fear" that reverses faith, not just the little fears we all face each day, but the mounting, persisting, tormenting type, that we fail to deal with as we know we should. Job said, "The thing I've greatly feared has come upon me." Job knew his mistake. He even spelt it out loud and clear! He was not confused or out of his mind. He knew what brought him down; his own fault.

There is no doubt that Job had originally had faith, but he allowed his faith to be swallowed up in fear. Sometimes we have to have faith in our faith - in the context of what faith can do versus what fear can achieve. It's in our own interest to stand in faith rather than fear. The fringe-benefits are much better!!

Charles Capps says, *"When you speak your fears they will grow and nullify your faith. You can't keep the devil from bringing thoughts of doubt and fear to your mind but those things will die unborn if we don't speak them."*[2] Our words either give our adversary or God, the license and opportunity to move on our behalf. And I know who I would prefer on my side!

King Solomon understood this when he said, *"Death and life are in the power of the tongue, and they who indulge in it shall eat the fruit of it [for death or life]" (Proverbs 18:21 AMPC)*, and in the New Testament it says, "For by your words you will be justified and acquitted, and by your words you will be condemned and sentenced" *(Matthew 12:37 AMPC)*. Ouch what a thought!

Many times however we don't realise the power of our words and the more we speak about negatives the more they grip our heart and multiply in strength. Fear will "establish" itself - taking as long as it takes - knowing that if it can establish a strong enough foot hold, any individual will eventually lose their strength and ability to deal with it. The same way that faith comes by hearing the word of God, fear comes by hearing negatives! Our words can create shields of defence or open-opportunities for evil intent.

We build and strengthen our shield *(hedge)* or we weaken it. For example, if we speak fear it insulates us and stops the blessings. Fear filled words produce more fear and invite the enemy to quench the blessings of God. *"He which soweth bountifully shall reap also bountifully"* (2 Corinthians 9:6).

It's good to remember that "everything" can work in its own "reverse-state." And bountiful words of "spoken-fear" can and will reap bountifully - after its own kind. On the other hand "whatever is born of God is victorious over the world; and this is the victory that conquers the world, even our faith" *(1 John 5:4 AMPC)*. We can be utterly victorious and unstoppable if we don't yield to fear.

Faith is stronger than fear and is our victory that overcomes the world; and principally comes through faith in God's Word. Heart faith comes from deep within where the Word abides. However we must remember, just because we have faith does not automatically mean that we will "operate" by that faith. Anything can be dormant and passive including our faith. We must have faith in the faith that we received from God; the very faith of the Son of God *(Galatians 2:20)*.

ENDNOTES:

1. Strong, James. S.T.D., L.L.D. 1890. Strong's Exhaustive Concordance, Dictionaries (Lexicon) of the Hebrew and Greek Words

2. "Fear is Faith in Reverse" by Charles Capps, online article, https://cappsministries.com/pages/fear-is-faith-in-reverse

3. This "Truth for the Journey" has been taken from: https://watchersofthe4kings.com

4. Unless otherwise indicated, all scripture references are taken from the King James Version of the Bible.

5. Scripture references marked AMPC are taken from the Amplified® Bible (AMPC), Copyright © 1954, 1958, 1962, 1964, 1965, 1987 by The Lockman Foundation. Used by permission. www.Lockman.org

6. Scripture references marked GW are taken from GOD'S WORD®, © 1995 God's Word to the Nations. Used by permission of Baker Publishing Group.

Letter 19

Truth for the Journey

The Perils of Disappointment

Letter to the Church, 13th August 2010

They trusted you and were never disappointed.
(Psalms 22:5 GW)

It's easy in this life to become disappointed; in fact who hasn't been at some point or another? Ministry in particular is an arena where disappointment can thrive! As a minister I had to learn a long time ago not to allow "disappointment" to get me down. It is all too easy to give into the "feelings" of disappointment, mainly where other people are involved *(especially when other ministers let you down!)* By measure of necessity, I learnt to get over disappointment as quickly as possible; the alternative is for un-forgiveness to set in which only taints our inner focus *(spiritual sight)* rendering us un-available to be used by God any longer.

Disappointment is *a firm fore-runner for un-forgiveness* and a sure tactic of our adversary who desires to get us over into disappointment for as long as possible so that un-forgiveness sets in. This of course traps us until we repent, but our enemy knows that many Christians have become so "dull" spiritually that they are totally unaware they are even walking in un-forgiveness.

Our opponent has watched the "human-experience" from the beginning of time and knows just where to "blind-side" us, especially using the realm of our emotions. At all costs we must keep our emotions in check - because this arena alone gives Satan all the opportunity he needs. If given an inch, he always takes a mile; we must not give him that opportunity.

There are many words that describe disappointment's character perfectly. In fact most words have at least one "synonym" *(descriptive word with identical meaning)*. The following are "synonyms" of disappointment: *dissatisfaction, displeasure, distress, discontent, disenchantment, disillusionment, frustration and regret.*

Anyone who has ever stepped into disappointment, even if just for a single day, will be familiar with these all too well! In fact I doubt there is a person alive who hasn't experienced all of them! 1 Corinthians 10:13 teaches us that there is no temptation that is not "common to all men," making it safe to assume that anyone and everyone has tasted this "bitter-pill" called "disappointment" at some point or another!

The Perils of Disappointment

We are all tempted to get into it because it's just like any other seductive temptation; we are lured into "disappointment" through "emotions" - but we must avoid this at any expense because it only leads to bitterness, which in turn leads to un-forgiveness which inadvertently costs us "everything."

From a personal front, some years ago my wife was deeply affected by "disappointment." I have said before, ministry is a breeding ground for this because some of the things that people are prepared to say or do at times - can be nothing short of "treachery!" Scripture is clear about treachery, in fact Isaiah said, "Traitors continue to betray, and their *treachery* grows worse and worse" *(Isaiah 24:16 GW)* and in Psalms 78:57 it says, "They were disloyal and *treacherous...* like arrows shot from a defective bow!" *(GW)*

Over a prolonged period of time, my wife had watched the behaviour of certain "respectable" people who lacked certain discretions and as a result she became increasingly "disillusioned" with all-things-ministry simply through this type of deep-seated "disappointment" that had lodged in her heart.

Harmless enough one might presume, but it did some damage, however thankfully she recovered; but there are many who don't. Actually there are many today who have left the ministry for this same reason and never returned. We are talking about reality here! None of us should give ourselves over to anything - because what starts with mere emotion ends up more critical - if left to germinate!

DAVID WAS GREATLY DISTRESSED

David knew this well, and he had reason to be distressed at times especially in 1 Samuel chapter 30:1-6 when after returning from the battlefield, he discovered that his own people were about to kill him! In addition, everything he owned was either burnt to the ground or taken captive *(kidnapped!)*

"David and his men came to the city, and, behold, *it was* burned with fire; and their wives, and their sons, and their daughters, were taken captives. Then David and the people that *were* with him lifted up their voice and wept, until they had no more power to weep" *(1 Samuel 30:3-4).*

In verse 6 we see David clearly distressed by the situation but instead of nervously "reacting" to the crisis we see him "responding" to it by faith; **"David was greatly distressed;** for the people spoke of stoning him, because the soul of all the people was grieved, every man for his sons and for his daughters: **but David encouraged himself in the** LORD **his God."**

Almost deranged with grief, David's own people had risen up against him with a united front, wanting to "exact-punishment" for their joint loss. In other words they wanted someone to blame and take their grief out upon. *(Note: the first rule of leadership "everything is your fault!")*

Now it's understandable that they did not want to party at this point, and they were themselves disappointed in David, perhaps they thought that his leadership or miss-management cost them everything? However, many of us at times have felt like the whole world was against us, which brought us great personal "distress." This is when we need to employ the same secret weapon that David had. An "inner-defence-mechanism" that would not allow the disappointments and stresses of life to overcome him. As over-comers, we too must learn to encourage ourselves in the Lord, to off-set the disappointments in our own lives *(Revelation 2:7, 11, 26; 3:5, 12, 21)*.

If the anointed kings of the bible had to keep themselves "encouraged" we are certainly not immune to the stresses of life, even with Christ on our side! It takes discipline and David would have developed this into his life, long "before" he ever went to battle.

Resisting disappointment is as much an "act-of-the-will" as is patience! These healthy "responses" to life sadly don't come to us naturally *(automatically)* instead we must work at them voluntarily until they "become" part of our natural responses to life. *(Remember our flesh is like a rebellious dog that must be tamed. Needing strong discipline until it's not necessary anymore!)*

DISAPPOINTMENT CAN DESTROY FAITH

Fundamentally and relationally "disappointment" means to fail to satisfy an expectation. Disappointment will always be on this earth, and as mentioned above, the most important thing is not what happens but how we "respond" to it! If allowed to affect us, disappointment has the ability to destroy our faith. It can make us angry at God, at others and at ourselves and can be all consuming.

I have met folks who are just so very angry "all" the time. The sad fact is that they experienced just one too many disappointments in their life - never overcame it - and as a result live angry with themselves and with the world *(everyone in it)* for the rest of their lives!

Faith can be consumed by this type of anger that comes from disappointment. I have seen people get so turned on to the Word of God and then when things don't work out as they had planned; disappointment sets in and their faith rapidly disappears. People can literally float on cloud nine for weeks until a "suddenly" occurs and then the disappointment bomb drops and their bubble bursts forever!

Disappointment can also cause many people to backslide. I have seen more people backslide through disappointment than anything else. People get disappointed in each other, and even turn their back on the Lord Jesus Christ because of it. But regardless of what anyone else does, the Word of God does not change and nor should we.

Then there are the "unfounded" or "imagined" disappointments; which are the same thing as "perceived-injury," something that I have taught on quite abundantly over the years because many people suffer from this; especially common in the Body of Christ!

Vain imaginations are the culprit, which make us "perceive" that people are doing us an injury when actually they are not. "Life-is-just-one-big-mind-game," one that we *must* win; we are over-comers in Christ. To achieve this we must first know His Word and not be willing to deviate from it, to the left hand or the right, because it's the only sure foundation we have. It offers us "pure-security" when the rest of the world is swimming with "disappointment, fear and insecurity."

Finally in Proverbs 31:27 it talks about the bread of discontent and self-pity! **"She looks well to how things go in her household, and the bread of idleness** (*gossip, discontent, and self-pity*) **she will not eat"** *(AMPC)*.

Discontentment means: unhappiness, irritation, annoyance, disapproval and anger. Disillusionment is similar in meaning to disappointment but also means: lack of expectation, cynicism and disenchantment. We must guard against these opponents of our faith.

ENDNOTES:

1. This "Truth for the Journey" has been taken from: https://watchersofthe4kings.com

2. Unless otherwise indicated, all scripture references are taken from the King James Version of the Bible.

3. Scripture references marked AMPC are taken from the Amplified® Bible (AMPC), Copyright © 1954, 1958, 1962, 1964, 1965, 1987 by The Lockman Foundation. Used by permission. www.Lockman.org

4. Scripture references marked GW are taken from GOD'S WORD®, © 1995 God's Word to the Nations. Used by permission of Baker Publishing Group.

Letter 20

Truth for the Journey

Worry is Practical Atheism

Letter to the Church, 2nd March 2010

Lord, I believe; help thou mine unbelief.
(Mark 9:24 KJV)

Do you work with someone, have a friend or a colleague who is always pessimistic and dampening your zeal of faith with their humanistic realism, doubt and unbelief? Perhaps you have an employee who points out what you don't have and why you can't do what you plan to do? They explain to you what you already know when you just ask them to do a job! The definition of a pessimist is someone who is gloomy and distrustful. However the definition for a cynic is *someone who knows everything and believes nothing!* Many people are cynical at heart; it is concealed and criticises faith at every turn.

In the world to be a pragmatist is a commendable quality, whereas in the world of faith it is where *all things practical start and all things spiritual stop!* Someone who is pragmatic is overly practical, lending too much emphasis to the flesh and the carnal mind.

Another character we often find ourselves working with *(rowing the boat with)* is the humanist! They are the ones who lend far too much to reason and all things natural while rejecting the importance of belief in God. They always look for the problems and the reasons why faith can't work! They magnify the problems above the solutions and drain you of mental, physical and spiritual energy. They work to lower your enthusiasm and inspiration. And if this type of person is your employee, you spend most of your time trying to keep them motivated and *"up"* all the time; so much so that you can never leave them to themselves otherwise they always manage to talk themselves out of a job! *I am talking about the average believer!*

WORRY AN UNDESIRABLE CHARACTER

Another undesirable character is that of worry... being over concerned, troubled, fretful and anxious. It is a bible sin! Especially prevalent right now when confidence in the global economy is zilch! *"...as goes the economy so goes the rest of the world."* But the bible warns us not to cast our confidence away, promising a reward to those who don't lose heart.

Pastor John Hagee said recently, **"Worry is practical atheism..!"** A definition of atheism is the *"...disbelief in or denial of the existence of God or gods."* And when we worry or lend too much thinking to the flesh we are literally *"denying God"* in the situation! Think of that... too many *believers* are actually *unbelievers!* I admire the father who said, *"Lord, I believe; help thou mine unbelief"* *(Mark 9:24 KJV).* At least he was honest and did not seek to cover it up! Maybe we should pray the same thing continually, *"Lord help me with my unbelief."*

> *He that overcometh shall inherit all things; and I will be his God, and he shall be my son. But the fearful, and unbelieving, and the abominable, and murderers, and whoremongers, and sorcerers, and idolaters, and all liars, shall have their part in the lake which burneth with fire and brimstone: which is the second death.*
> *(Revelation 21:7-8 KJV)*

At times I have described myself as a *"realist"* yet in the positive sense; as I usually *say things for what they are...* but not at the *expense* of faith... Either we *see* things as the flesh reveals them or as God reveals them. We must be seers by the Spirit of God and not our own flesh.

Carefully *choose* who you have working around you, however if the choice is *not* yours, then learn to insulate yourself! Because those who lean towards these characteristics will always be looking for the negatives and always busy trying to work everything out; calculating the impossibilities before you have even had chance to believe that the best might happen...!

Usually those operating in such behaviour suffer with rejection and do not have a revelation of who *they* are in

Christ... *(an orphan spirit)* but if you have truly met Christ, and He has been revealed to your heart... then you will never worry again!

If He is the answer, what's the problem? If He says yes then who can say no?

Your heavenly Father will take care of every issue for your life, as He is more aware than we, of the things that we need.

ENDNOTES:

1. This "Truth for the Journey" has been taken from: https://watchersofthe4kings.com
2. Scripture references marked KJV are taken from the King James Version of the Bible.

LETTER 21

Truth for the Journey

Happiness Begins Between Your Ears

Letter to the Church, 26th February 2010

This one thing I do ... I press toward the mark...
(Philippians 3:13-14 KJV)

Personally I enjoy watching people *succeed* in this life; excelling in their God given purpose; increasing and growing in their knowledge of Him, as they continue walking in obedience. There's nothing more tragic than the unanswered call or the untapped potential, this grieves the Spirit of God inside of me. Just how much does God enjoy watching over our development!

In the same way that the artist treasures his painting or the master craftsman admires his work; so too our Creator cherishes us. He always has our best interests at heart; our dreams, goals, well-being and quality of life. All of which He intended for us to enjoy, so long as we live within the boundary of THE MIND OF CHRIST!

The fact is this; if we have the mind of Christ, we will adopt an excellent lifestyle; which is not for the weary! It is keenly developed on a daily basis incorporating our speech, thoughts and actions; our spirit, soul and body. The collective meaning for the word conduct is: behaviour, manner, ways, carry out, accomplish, perform, demeanour.

THE MIND IS A CALDRON POT OF IDEAS

Every one of us, by the time we reach adulthood, have developed a personal set of ethos *(inner rules, codes of conduct, philosophies)*. The experiences of formative years shape our emotional infrastructure and complex systems of self defence... *survival of the fittest!*

Yet in learning to *survive* we also learn to *self-destruct!* And those very complex infrastructures within us have all got to be changed, once we meet Christ. The mind is a caldron pot of ideas which develops its own shape *through generational, sociological and political influences including basic family semantics!* And has all got to be *transformed* into a new shape and demeanour that spells, *"Christ."* Clearly it is *not* possible to know Him and remain the same!

We discover that our flawed systems of personal defence are totally *inadequate* and our sources of collective advice are completely bankrupt in comparison. Instead the realization of our total *necessity* for a Saviour meets us head-on; our need for Him to be *Lord and Master* to whom we can give final control. Allowing Him alone to *shape our morals and ideas and navigate our inner compass!*

The answer can only be, *"the Word and the Spirit of God within us."* As Christians we have the opportunity to be revolutionized and transformed inwardly upon knowing Christ. The evidence of which is to be substantiated through our outward behaviour and influence on the world and culture around us.

Regeneration is instant but renewal of the mind takes time. Sanctification is a lifelong process, a critical transition involving the continual laying off the carnal mind and taking on *(learning to yield to)* the Mind of Christ; *sanctification is to be set apart and made holy.* Our minds are intended for holy use, and should not *"wonder out of the presence of God."* Something quite hard to achieve in this day and age; but with the fruit self control it can be done!

Renewal is a lengthy process, requiring much more than isolated efforts of bible study! It takes dedicated self adjustment learning to think like Christ!

Many Christians are incapacitated because they do not know how to protect their thought lives. Satan will bombard us with confusion, fear, hatred, suspicion, depression, mistrust and a host of other mental distractions.

Someone once said, *"Happiness begins between your ears and your mind is the drawing room for tomorrow's circumstances..."* Remember, what happens in your mind will happen in time and therefore one of our first priorities must be *mind-management*.

ENDNOTES:

1. This "Truth for the Journey" has been taken from: https://watchersofthe4kings.com
2. Scripture references marked KJV are taken from the King James Version of the Bible.

Letter 22

Truth for the Journey

Every Situation and Circumstance

Letter to the Church, 14th April 2010

*W*ho through faith conquered kingdoms, administered justice, and gained what was promised...

(Hebrews 11:33)

We can all admit that instead of confessing God's truth at times, we do nothing but complain. How many times have we said, *"Lord I want to quit, I can't carry on like this..."* because we have found ourselves living by the *"just get-by gospel"* rather than the *"overcoming gospel!"* Some people are genuinely satisfied with just existing from day to day, but this is not God's plan.

And although we live in the kingdoms of this world, we are called to administer the justice of a completely different Kingdom. In order to fully comprehend our opening scripture, let us dissect it a little while. For instance what does it mean exactly to administer justice? Literally from the Greek it means: *to toil, labour and work for, be committed to and minister about (justice)*. And justice here chiefly refers to righteousness.

Still it's interesting that the writers of the NIV chose to use the English word "**administer** justice" *(in place of "wrought righteousness" as used in the KJV)* which in our language has a whole host of meanings such as: conduct, control, execute; direct, superintend, supervise, oversee, rule. Distribute, supply and furnish; all of which puts a more interesting edge on it.

So then we could define "administering justice" using the English language as simply: distributing and executing righteousness! Or supervising and executing the rule of righteousness on the earth. And it is for this express reason that we did not jump straight to "GO," collect $200 and go straight to heaven *(on this monopoly board of life)* as soon as we got saved, because who else would continue His mission of administering justice and distributing righteousness on the earth - if not us?

Why else are we here and why else are we empowered by His Holy Spirit? Just so we can speak with other tongues? No! Heaven forbid! Oh how much more Pentecost and the marvellous baptism of the Holy Spirit mean than just that!

Nor does our main objective as believers just consists of getting saved and then existing in a state of spiritual inertia for the rest of our lives; co-existing with the world in some kind of juxtaposition - of "them and us, believers vs. non-believers." No! We have a job to do. We have had our defining moment His name is Christ, our crucified and resurrected Lord. He left His mark on this world. They can't rightly forget that, no matter how hard they still try.

No politician or celebrity throughout the ages, from Hercules to Stalin has ever out-ranked, out-smarted or out-lived the name of Jesus! His influence on planet earth goes from generation to generation long after those other names have long expired! The name of Jesus will never quietly just disappear into oblivion! Even when overt persecution doesn't successfully quash His name and deception is deployed against believers instead - His name still lives on..!

And our job as believers does not just involve soliciting converts but also creating disciples who will give themselves over to living righteously and spreading God's Word and righteousness throughout the earth, "as he is, even so are we in this world" *(1 John 4:17 ASV)*. We are to multiply ourselves and to populate the earth and to influence every situation with His righteousness. The influence of His Kingdom on this earth "...is not a matter of eating and drinking, but of righteousness, peace and joy in the Holy Spirit" *(Romans 14:17)*.

However this produces a lightning effect - a direct hit! Light colliding with the darkness and precisely why persecution occurs *(John 17:14-15)*, they are two separate kingdoms and each is hostile to the other: "For the sinful nature is always hostile to God" *(Romans 8:7 NLT)*. It's a direct clash. But the clash brings change. The saltiness brings flavour. And righteousness brings salvation and justification *(Matthew 5:13)*.

DON'T BE EJECT BUTTON MINDED!

So in order to summarize: "to declare and administer justice..." means that we should keep on keeping on - preaching the gospel till the very end. No matter how tough it gets. Reflect on this for a moment... many folks are busying themselves these days trying to figure out when the rapture is going to happen and whether or not they will escape the tribulation to come.

They have all their pre-trib, mid-trib and post-trib theories wrapped up! But most of that is bent on self preservation. Why? Because the fact eludes them that persecution is already here *(and has never left)*; in many countries of this world today vast numbers of people are suffering terribly for their faith and the rapture has not rescued them yet!

We have to avoid transforming this gospel into a westernized man-made religion, where we can press the "Eject Button" whenever it suits us. If that were possible many throughout history would have pressed that "Rapture Now" button long before now - if it was in their hands to do so, but of course it was not! In fact each generation has had its own take on the rapture. And the more and more we humanize it, to make it fit the political correctness of our day, the more it loses its proper meaning and significance and all we end up with is a religion that has been denied of its own power. "... having a form of godliness, but denying the power thereof..." *(2 Timothy 3:5 KJV)*

Our consolidation can be drawn from this, that while we know the darkness is getting darker, the light is getting brighter and we overcome with the blood of the Lamb and word of our testimony; this is our legitimate close and divine epilogue, where evil is truly and utterly overcome with good in and through our lives every single day! *(Romans 12:21; Revelation 12:11; Colossians 1:12)*

ENDNOTES:

1. This "Truth for the Journey" has been taken from: https://watchersofthe4kings.com
2. Unless otherwise indicated, all scripture references are taken from the HOLY BIBLE, NEW INTERNATIONAL VERSION ®. NIV ®. Copyright © 1973, 1978, 1984 by the International Bible Society. Used by permission of Zondervan Publishing House. All rights reserved.
3. Scripture references marked ASV are taken from the American Standard Version of the bible.
4. Scripture references marked KJV are taken from the King James Version of the Bible.
5. Scripture quotations marked NLT are taken from the Holy Bible, New Living Translation, copyright © 1996, 2004, 2007 by Tyndale House Foundation. Used by permission of Tyndale House Publishers, Inc., Carol Stream, Illinois 60188. All rights reserved.

Letter 23

Truth for the Journey

God's X-ray Vision

Letter to the Church, 3rd August 2010

Many people noticed the signs he was displaying and, seeing they pointed straight to God, entrusted their lives to him. But Jesus didn't entrust his life to them. He knew them inside and out... He didn't need any help in seeing right through them.
(John 2:23-25 MSG)

The "extreme" tends to surround the prophetic ministry. People either love or hate the prophet! Things get very black and white around them. People either keep a safe distance in fear of what they might discover or go to the other extreme and become "groupies" who hang on every word! Still genuine prophets can evoke much respect from people and make them feel slightly nervous because they give this sense that they can see straight through people which provokes a little insecurity!

However it must be said, no matter how genuine a prophet is, they cannot see everything; in fact "nothing" unless God reveals it to them. And all of us are warned against using our own "vain imaginations" *(Acts 4:25; Romans 1:21).*

But God planned it that the prophet was a blessing and not a curse! In fact a true and "seasoned" prophet is very quiet, not willing to speak at all, until God reveals something to him. Prophets are serious folks, not given to chatty or easy "small-talk," because they are literally "mouth-pieces" for God. And with the severe "testing" they endure to keep them "pure" *(especially where their mouths are concerned),* they fear God too much to have a "loose-mouth." They know that they must not try to speak in regards to the flesh one minute and for God the next, *(salt water and fresh cannot come from the same fountain! See James 3:12).*

Also and most importantly God is not in the business of revealing "everything" about "everybody" all the time. Revealing everybody's "dirty washing" achieves nothing, even for His prophets. God has only our "best-interests" at heart. Therefore we can be secure that "no" prophet, no matter how seasoned they claim to be, can see "everything." God's purpose for the prophetic ministry exceeds and is much bigger than that!

PROPHETS ARE HUMAN AND MAKE MISTAKES

So even if the prophet has the ability to know the intents and purposes of men's hearts more than others, "to err is still human!" Prophets are definitely human and still make mistakes, just as Samuel did in 1 Samuel 16:7 where God told him, "Don't judge by his appearance or height, for I have rejected him. The LORD doesn't see things the way you see them. People judge by outward appearance, but the LORD looks at the heart" *(NLT)*.

Needless to say that "knowing everything about everyone" would be hard to bear for any prophet. They would end up feeling like Elijah did who desperately wanted to "eject" and leave all the backslidden folks behind!

The prophetic ministry at its "best" has the anointing to lead people quickly to repentance. Everything becomes "clear" when the prophet genuinely speaks for God. The choices in front of people become crystal clear; heaven or hell, rebellion or submission, spirit or flesh! Needless to say that this type of ministry provokes a reaction wherever it goes; those who are stubborn and rebellious rise up and refuse to choose, while on the other hand those who are humble in heart, are totally set free!

Having said all this, it is still through the prophetic that true "motives" can be revealed to everyone. The Young's Literal Translation says in Proverbs 26:24-26, "By his lips doth a hater dissemble, and in his heart he placeth deceit, when his voice is gracious trust not in him, for seven abominations [are] in his heart. Hatred is covered by deceit, ***revealed is its wickedness in an assembly.***" A good example of this is when God used Peter with a strong prophetic anointing and exposed the deceit of Ananias and his wife.

Hatred, deceit, guile, falsehood and wickedness are all things that can be concealed in the heart and in church life; until it is revealed. This is the job of the prophet. To "reveal" and to "clean up" no one else is able to see into the hearts of people like the prophet.

There are lots of pastors who would have welcomed Ananias and Sapphira with open arms, as a supportive couple and would have gladly benefited from their generous financial support - but *not* the apostle or prophet! Rather it was through the prophetic ministry of Peter that their true "motives" were "revealed" to the entire congregation, ***"revealed is its wickedness in an assembly"*** *(Proverbs 26:26 YLT).*

With this prophetic anointing and the gift of discerning of spirits, Peter was able to see what most others could not see; the deceit that had filled their hearts. Satan sugar coats his deception after all, but it did not fool the apostle or prophet! In fact it is the job of the prophetic to "clear out, clean up, put in order and point the way" like no other ministry gift can. They are not caught up with the "petty," and swiftly deal with anything that has the potential to hinder the development of the "whole."

Many will claim to be doing "fine" when in actual fact they are a poor spiritual mess! For this reason the office of a prophet is feared by many and literally "hated" by some. Nevertheless if permitted to function as a prophet should, the consequences can only be sheer blessing, and for a church to grow with any kind of strength, it is vital for believers to "live" in the light and not just be entertained!

We can pretend to be holy and behave sanctimoniously with the world around us, while the underlying problems are eating us up. The prophet however has the ability to draw people rapidly out of their sin. But only those who are willing respond to their type of message, others are usually hostile. Since those who are not willing to be "freed" of their sin, often "defend & protect" it instead!

GOD NEEDS A MOUTHPIECE

So it's not a popular job for the prophet and usually is not a job for the volunteer! But God is faithful to His prophets, as we see here, "He suffered no man to do them wrong: yea, he reproved kings for their sakes, Saying, *Touch not mine anointed, and do my prophets no harm...*" *(1 Chronicles 16:21-22 KJV, also Psalms 105:15)*

In addition, the prophet's true position is not one of "judgment," but of "help." Therefore if a prophet has no interest in people whatsoever, God knows just how to deal with them just as He did with Jonah who, **"rose up to flee... from being in the presence of the Lord [as His prophet]"** *(Jonah 1:3 AMPC).* God rescued Jonah from his consequences only after he re-submitted himself back to God and dealt with his own rebellion!

In truth God has a mandate and His prophets "must" follow that objective. They are not called to go their "own" way or do their "own" thing, or even use their "own" voice to herald with... instead they literally become God's "mouthpiece" and have been used by Him throughout the ages to prophecy about Jesus Christ; coming to earth and then later returning again; with times of refreshing following for all those who believe until the restoration of all things...

In Acts 3:19-23 "The Message Bible" says it like this, "Now it's time to change your ways! **Turn to face God so he can wipe away your sins, pour out showers of blessing to refresh you,** and send you the Messiah he prepared for you, namely, Jesus. For the time being he must remain out of sight in heaven **until everything is restored to order again just the way God, through the preaching of his holy prophets of old, said it would be.**

Moses for instance said, 'Your God will raise up for you a prophet just like me from your family. Listen to every word he speaks to you. Every last living soul who refuses to listen to that prophet will be wiped out from the people.'"

Finally the main objective, "the prophetic" has to be "a blessing" and not "a curse." Therefore anyone who claims to be a prophet today; yet is angry, negative or bitter towards people all the time; is not operating in their true capacity and God will inevitably "silence them," *(because the damage they are capable of is irreparable!)*

Consequently the prophet's main job is one of "communicating" the heart of God; which is a communication that must not be "misinterpreted" or "perverted" and certainly not by any "lack-of-character" from His prophets. First and foremost God uses "willingness and obedience;" only then can true blessings come upon everyone! *(Isaiah 1:19-20)*

Lastly, the prophetic ministry operates best in conjunction with the ministry of an Apostle, as seen with Peter mentioned above. And in these *(last)* days in particular, we will not only see the other gifts operating with increasing authority, but we will especially witness the prophetic and apostolic gifts working together in vast power and governing authority. This ensures that together they accomplish God's agenda of not only "tearing down" deceptions but also "building-up" all things concerning God's "Kingdom & His Righteousness" *(Matthew 6:33)*.

ENDNOTES:

1. This "Truth for the Journey" has been taken from: https://watchersofthe4kings.com

2. Scripture references marked AMPC are taken from the Amplified® Bible (AMPC), Copyright © 1954, 1958, 1962, 1964, 1965, 1987 by The Lockman Foundation. Used by permission. www.Lockman.org

3. Scripture references marked KJV are taken from the King James Version of the Bible.

4. Scripture quotations marked MSG are taken from The Message. Copyright © 1993, 1994, 1995, 1996, 2000, 2001, 2002. Used by permission of NavPress Publishing Group.

5. Scripture quotations marked NLT are taken from the Holy Bible, New Living Translation, copyright © 1996, 2004, 2007 by Tyndale House Foundation. Used by permission of Tyndale House Publishers, Inc., Carol Stream, Illinois 60188. All rights reserved.

6. Scripture quotations marked YLT are taken from the Young's Literal Translation of the bible.

Letter 24

Truth for the Journey

We are the Prophet of our Own Lives!

Letter to the Church, 6th August 2010

*O**ut of the abundance of the heart the mouth speaketh... every idle word that men shall speak, they shall give account... For by thy words thou shalt be justified, and by thy words thou shalt be condemned.*

(Matthew 12:34-37)

As already mentioned in Letter 16, God created us to be the "prophet of our own lives." This means that our destiny is within our own mouths! There is no one else to blame. It's our own words - not anyone else's - that determine our successes or failures in this life; "...if thou shalt confess with thy mouth the Lord Jesus, and shalt believe in thine heart that God hath raised him from the dead, thou shalt be saved. For with the heart man believeth unto righteousness; and with the mouth confession is made unto salvation" *(Romans 10:9-10)*. In fact our words either bring good things to pass or wicked. The decision is ours.

It is true to say that God has never and will never do "anything" without "speaking" about it first! This could be called a "spiritual law." In fact in Genesis 1:1-29 we can see "nine" consecutive times during the creation process where it says "God said." He "spoke" over His creation until He was fully satisfied! We too must keep speaking over our lives; not once but many times; until we see completion in those areas we need it the most and then move on.

We must do as He does, God releases His faith by His Words! 1 John 4:17 says; "...as he is, so are we in this world" therefore we must operate the same way. We know this is possible because we have been given the "God kind of faith" that Jesus spoke of in Mark 11:22!

This "God kind of faith" is not limited. It can do what God does with it, as long as we operate in it as He does! This takes understanding and lots of willingness because this type of faith is not subject to human emotion but is "long suffering" and will keep speaking at a mountain until it moves! Even the best educated guess can't know exactly how long it took for the "creation process" to take place, as mentioned in Genesis chapter one.

Six mere days in scripture can mean something entirely different in our concept of "real-time!" For instance some scholars believe that between each verse of Genesis One; "many" consecutive years were represented. This is very plausible, considering what it says in 2 Peter 3:8 *"...one day is with the Lord as a thousand years, and a thousand years as one day!"*

SPOKEN WORDS ARE A CREATIVE FORCE

As I have already pointed out above, God spoke directly to His creation nine separate times in just one chapter, so evidently God had a lot to SAY during the process! But faith does require "words" to operate and nothing has changed. In fact WORDS still have a great deal of involvement in what we create today. Words are still a much "creative-force" for good or for evil right now. It's worth thinking about... Selah!

Then to further drive home the point about the need for us to "behave" like God specifically where faith is concerned, Ephesians 5:1 tells us to be "imitators" of God just as children would imitate their parents. And in order for us to properly "imitate" Him this would mean for us to *talk* like Him, *act* like Him and even *think* like Him. And speaking to things is what God does and so must we!

This does not just apply to us, Jesus also operated by such faith principles while he was on earth *(see Mark 11:23; Matthew 17:20).* For instance He spoke to the wind and the sea. He spoke to demons. He spoke to the fig tree. He even spoke to dead men! They all "obeyed" His *SPOKEN WORDS...* meaning His faith filled words had great power and influence, just as ours should.

Truly I say to you, if you have faith [that is living] like a grain of mustard seed, you can say to this mountain, Move from here to yonder place, and it will move; and nothing will be impossible to you.
(Matthew 17:20 AMPC)

God was in the business of releasing His faith through His words and we must follow suit. But admittedly our words are usually loaded with a mixture of fear and faith with life and death. The mixture is the danger point because salt water and fresh cannot be poured out of the same fountain. We are obligated to speak life! *(See Genesis 1:3).*

Again, if Jesus could imitate His Father and get the same results, so can we! In John 14:12 Jesus said, *"He that believeth on me the works that I do shall he do also; and greater..."* These principles of faith are based on spiritual laws which work for whosoever applies them and sets them in motion.

Just consider it more closely; who really wants all their negative words to literally come to pass? No one right?! And those who truly perceive that everything they "say" has the potential of coming-to-pass just as they "spoke," swiftly change their vocabulary! But this takes revelation *(renewing of the mind)* and a lot of assistance from the Holy Spirit!

SPOKEN WORDS PROGRAM OUR SPIRIT

Spoken words program our spirit *(heart)* either towards success or defeat. **Words are truly containers; carrying the ability to produce whatever they contain just like a seed;** "...faith cometh by hearing and hearing by the Word of God" *(Romans 10:17).*

Faith comes more quickly when we hear ourselves quoting, speaking, and saying the same things God says. It is a fact that all of us we will more readily receive God's Word into our spirits by *hearing ourselves speaking it...* than if we hear someone else speaking it. This brings us to the major role that "confession" takes in our faith walk. In fact throughout the New Testament there are four basic kinds of confessions that exist and we will look at them just quickly as follows below:

The Confession of Repentance: The first confession found in the New Testament is the confession of sin taught by John the Baptist and Jesus to the Jewish people in their day. This act of confession however, is not what we know today as Christian repentance. Actually, the confession of sin and water baptism that we read about in Matthew 3 and Luke 3 was an act by the people of Israel under the Abrahamic *(or Old)* Covenant.

Prior to Jesus going to the cross, the Jews knew what it was to confess their sins and repent, but their sins were only "covered" in atonement by the blood of an animal which was sacrificed once a year. It wasn't until the sacrifice of Jesus' blood that sin could actually be wiped out and not just covered up *(see Hebrews 10)*.

The Confession of Salvation: is the confession of a sinner. It's what we now know as the prayer of salvation. In John 16, Jesus explained that the Spirit would come to convict *"the world"* of sin and basically the confession of a sinner under the New Covenant is simply that Jesus is Lord! "The word is nigh thee, even in thy mouth, and in thy heart:

that is, the word of faith, which we preach; that **if thou shalt confess with thy mouth the Lord Jesus, and shalt believe in thine heart that God hath raised Him from the dead, thou shalt be saved"** *(Romans 10:8-9).*

The Confession of Sin: Christians also must confess their sins, especially those who step out of fellowship with the Father. The bible says that if you have sin in your life to confess it. 1 John 1:9 says, "If we confess our sins, he is faithful and just to forgive us our sins, and to cleanse us from all unrighteousness." The moment sin is confessed, is the same moment it is gotten rid of. By faith, we spewed it out of our mouths and God was faithful and just to forgive us of it and to cleanse us.

The Confession of Faith in God's Word involves our faith in Christ as our High Priest. Paul wrote *"...consider the Apostle and High Priest of our confession, Christ Jesus" (Hebrews 3:1 NKJV).* This word "confession" in the Greek actually means, "saying the same thing as; saying what God says." This makes the act of "confession" nothing more than a spoken "affirmation" of bible truth which is repeating the very things God has already said in His Word and believing them at the same time.

To finish, this principle of faith that works hand in hand with our confession will never change. Faith operates by believing what we say and saying what we believe and doing so over and over again - in line with God's Word - for the rest of our lives. A process that helps bring salvation and every other thing that God has promised us.

We are the Prophet of our Own Lives!

ENDNOTES:

1. This "Truth for the Journey" has been taken from: https://watchersofthe4kings.com

2. Unless otherwise indicated, all scripture references are taken from the King James Version of the Bible.

3. Scripture references marked AMPC are taken from the Amplified® Bible (AMPC), Copyright © 1954, 1958, 1962, 1964, 1965, 1987 by The Lockman Foundation. Used by permission. www.Lockman.org

4. Scripture references marked NKJV are taken from the New King James Version. Copyright © 1982 by Thomas Nelson, 1982 by Thomas Nelson, Inc. Used by permission. All rights reserved.

Letter 25

Truth for the Journey

Don't Speak until God Gives you the Key

Letter to the Church, 10th August 2010

Wherefore, holy brethren, partakers of the heavenly calling, consider the Apostle and High Priest of our profession, Christ Jesus.
(Hebrews 3:1)

My wife recently reminded me of a story that a pastor once told us when in Entebbe, Uganda. He told us how he had a kennel full of dogs. He chose two of these dogs and spoke life to one and death to the other - continually for a period of time. After just weeks one of those dogs began to slowly die. Then the pastor felt sorry for the dog and began to speak words of life over it instead, but it was too late. Death had taken hold and that dog sadly died. What a crude and cruel experiment you might say. But this pastor found out, in this somewhat rudimentary way, the extent of his words. Evidently our words cause a "reaction" no matter what, for good or for bad.

Dr. Mike Murdock in his book, **"Wisdom for Winning"** says, "One friend noted an inner depression when he indulged in revealing the flaws of others: *'The words of a talebearer are as wounds...' (Proverbs 18:8)* God brought healing through the Word: *'Whoso keepeth his mouth and his tongue keepeth his soul from troubles' (Proverbs 21:23).*" He goes on to say to guard your conversations.[1]

Jesus can only use our faith filled words to fulfil His purposes. Any other words we speak will be judged. Matthew 12:36 says that we will be judged for "every idle *(or careless)* word that we speak."

In fact the International Standard Bible Encyclopedia *(ISBE)* states that the Greek word *(argós)* generally used for *"idle or idleness"* in the New Testament literally meant, *inactive, useless, empty gossip, nonsensical talk.*[2] Whereas the Strong's Concordance #G692 takes *argos (pronounced ar-gos')* as generally meaning, *inactive, unemployed; lazy, useless; barren, idle or slow.*[3]

THE APOSTLE OF OUR PROFESSION

So this means that Jesus will either use or only judge our words. With this in mind James warns that if our tongue is unbridled it can actually *"...sets on fire the course of our life, and is set on fire by Hell" (James 3:6).* In Hebrews 3:1 however we are instructed to; *"Consider the Apostle and High Priest of our profession, Christ (or the Anointed One) Jesus" (emphasis added)* and the word translated as "profession" in that verse can also be translated as "confession." This means that God appointed Jesus to be our High Priest, only over our confession - which is our "declaration of FAITH."

Having said all this; both our words - faith filled words and our words of idleness have affected our lives up to this point. In fact we could say that our lives today are the "direct-result" of our own consistent choice of words. So perhaps now's the time to change our vocabulary, especially those who don't like themselves very much!

True to His Word, Jesus Christ as the Apostle and High Priest will faithfully back our words - but only when we speak what God says in His Word. Think about it, God placed such a high premium on "words" purely because He can only "agree" with His own Word in our mouths, and this is what He wants to bring to pass. It is a total revelation to some that mere "words" can be so literally powerful that they can change the very course of our eternal destiny.

As Christians we have an "out-and-out" obligation to speak "right words" and what a difference they can make! We all know that from the very beginning of our experience with Christ, we came head to head with the power of words and the awesome difference that they can make, *"...if thou shalt confess with thy mouth the Lord Jesus, and shalt believe in thine heart that God hath raised him from the dead, thou shalt be saved" (Romans 10:9).*

Many people around the world now confess faith in Jesus as their Lord and Saviour and proclaim that God had raised Him from the dead and as a result are no longer hell bound, but heaven bound! Mere "words" mingled with truth and faith changed their eternal destiny forever. But we must also consider that if words can change destiny, words can also change anything!

There is "power" in words. In fact the spiritual forces of life or death are "released" through our words alone. This means that "beyond" our conversion experience we must continue to make the right choices with our words! Knowing God's Word is essential for this. And by speaking "right Words" like this we can help steer the course that God wants us to take; knowing every word we speak will affect everyone else around us; for good or for bad.

What an awesome responsibility we have! All the idle and fruitless chatter we once enjoyed is now a privilege we can no longer indulge ourselves! For when we committed ourselves to Christ we also committed our mouths to Him. This we can never change; our mouths are too significant to trifle with; either they are fountains of life or death, blessing or cursing, something becomes too serious to be jovial about, especially as one matures in Christ. We are totally accountable.

THE HOLY SPIRIT GIVES LIFE TO HIS WORD

Once again Jesus is not committed to "any" words that we speak; only to spoken-words of faith that agree with His, and as High Priest of our confession *(spoken faith in His Word)*, Jesus becomes obligated to **bring-those-words-to-pass**, but let me point out that it is the Holy Spirit who **brings-them-to-LIFE.** We see this in John 6:63 where it says; "It is the Spirit Who gives life [He is the Life-giver]; the flesh conveys no benefit whatever [there is no profit in it]. The words *(truths)* that I have been speaking to you are spirit and life" *(AMPC).*

The very words that Jesus spoke were inspired and brought to life by the Holy Spirit, how much more do we need the help! **So our High Priest and the Holy Spirit work together,** to bring our words to life and to pass! "...the word is very near you, in your mouth and in your mind and in your heart, so that you can do it" *(Deuteronomy 30:14, also Romans 10:8).*

Then 1 Corinthians 1:4-5 also tells us that Jesus "enriches our utterance." That is, He takes our words of faith and enriches them with His. So no matter how we look at it, **the words we speak have the ability to carry the very creative force of Almighty God behind them.** What weight that is! And they are "bound" to come to pass! "I thank my God... Jesus Christ; that in everything ye are enriched by him, in all utterance, and in all knowledge..."

As mentioned in the last *"Truth for the Journey,"* God intended us to be the "prophet of our own lives," so that we could bring good things to pass by using our mouths to "affirm" His word. "...out of the abundance of the heart the mouth speaketh. A good man out of the good treasure of the heart ***bringeth forth*** good things..." *(Matthew 12:34-37)*

It's evident therefore that an opportunity exists to all of us; to ***bring forth*** life or to ***bring forth*** death. Some people imagine that their words don't *"bring forth"* anything! But for those of us who understand differently and have had this "revealed" to us by the Holy Spirit, now have a responsibility to act upon what we know.

For the rest of our lives we must act wisely - every single time we open our mouths! No longer can we leisurely engage in idle chatter. On the other hand we can still be spontaneous and free - sure! - but with "restraint" and self control, knowing that EVERY word will be judged.

To finish I heard Ulf Ekman once say, **"Put a padlock on your mouth and only speak when God gives you the key!"**

ENDNOTES:

1. "Wisdom for Winning" by Mike Murdock. Copyright © 1988. Published by Honor Books. Printed in USA, p164

2. Orr, James. M.A., D.D., General Editor, ISBE - International Standard Bible Encyclopedia; e-Sword ® version 7.6.1 Copyright © 2000-2005. All Rights Reserved. Registered trade mark of Rick Meyers. Equipping Ministries Foundation. USA www.e-sword.net

3. Strong, James. S.T.D., L.L.D. 1890. Strong's Exhaustive Concordance, Dictionaries (Lexicon) of the Hebrew and Greek Words

4. This "Truth for the Journey" has been taken from: https://watchersofthe4kings.com

5. Unless otherwise indicated, all scripture references are taken from the King James Version of the Bible.

6. Scripture references marked AMPC are taken from the Amplified® Bible (AMPC), Copyright © 1954, 1958, 1962, 1964, 1965, 1987 by The Lockman Foundation. Used by permission. www.Lockman.org

LETTER 26

Truth for the Journey

Spirit and Word

Letter to the Church, 31st August 2010

For the Word of God is LIVING and ACTIVE...
(Hebrews 4:12 NIV)

The first time we ever see a "birth" taking place in scripture is in Genesis chapter one. The first thing that was ever "brought to birth" was the very Word of God! God "spoke" and then that Word had to be "created." This process involved not only time but also three intrinsic elements; **"brooding, speaking, and creating."** Incidentally this "process" has never ceased. *(God still does all three! And we will look at this here).* As for the "brooding or hovering" which the scriptures use to describe the Spirit's "behaviour" during creation - almost explains a period not unlike "incubation" where the Spirit appears protective, caring and patient - but in readiness to ACT.

Let's see this unfold in Genesis chapter one where the Amplified Bible says; "IN THE beginning God *(prepared, formed, fashioned, and)* created the heavens and the earth. [Hebrews 11:3.] The earth was without form and an empty waste, and darkness was upon the face of the very great deep.

The Spirit of God was moving (*hovering, brooding*) over the face of the waters" *(Genesis 1:1-2 AMPC)*. Consequently "brooding, hovering or moving," are all descriptive words that help portray the Spirit's; "eagerness," "willingness" and even "promptness" but certainly not slothfulness! He did not fall asleep in other words - waiting for God to speak!

Deuteronomy 32:11-12 *(GW)* also mentions this divine-instinct of God; "Like an eagle that stirs up its nest, **hovers over** its young, spreads its wings to catch them, and carries them on its feathers, so the LORD alone led his people." Therefore brooding or hovering is definitely something that God does *(by His Spirit)* not lastly during creation; hovering eagerly and willingly - always ready to perform the truth of His Word.

Today this process of "brooding, speaking and creating" is still the same. The only difference being - that now God's Word is in "our" mouths. He still wants to create His Word and bring it to pass; **"...these words are very near you. They're in your mouth and in your heart..."** *(Deuteronomy 30:14 GW)* So just as God "spoke" His Word in Genesis, we also must speak out His creative Word now!

Spirit and Word

THE SPIRIT OF GOD MUST BE PRESENT

The Authorized Version says that after, **"the Spirit of God moved..."** **"God said."** In fact during this creation scene of Genesis chapter one - we can see **"God said"** no less than ten consecutive times. The Spirit hovered, God spoke, created, saw, named and blessed. But our emphasis today is on what came first; "brooding/hovering, speaking and creating." **The Spirit of God must be "present,"** His Word **must be "spoken"** and His creative power "released."

Notice that the brooding/hovering of the Spirit only lasted "until" the Word was "spoken." Then it was time to ACT. This ultimately means that the Spirit needs "instruction!" In fact He is still bringing this "instruction" to birth today through our lives.

For this reason we are taking this lengthy look at the Holy Spirit's behaviour surrounding the "speaking" of God's Word, because it is vital to its being "brought to life." This subject in fact could be looked at from many different angles and we could draw from a myriad of different scriptures to bring it to a conclusion. However I just want to look briefly at this original Hebrew word *(rāḥap Strong's #H7363)*[1] which was used to explain precisely what the Spirit's "conduct" was during the creation; perhaps you see something here that you have not seen before as I did!

To "brood/hover/move" on the face of the deep - came from a primitive root; to *brood;* and by implication means to *be relaxed:* flutter, move or shake. Again these words are "descriptive" of a bird "nesting" but I want to focus-in-on-the-word "relaxed" for a moment here. Before I saw this in my own personal study, I had never previously imagined the creation process *(whether before, during or after)* as being remotely relaxing! More like hard work, that required a concluding day of "rest" *(even for God!)*

My point is this: if the Holy Spirit was "relaxing" while "brooding" at the same time, this means that He was not "fretting" *(trying to force-something-to-happen)* rather He was patiently trusting and waiting for the Word *(Christ's instruction to "act" upon)*. The Holy Spirit always acts to "enhance" the Word!

Perhaps some people imagine the Holy Spirit during the creation-scene as being much like an unloaded "spring," who was "released" to perform the Word of God; possibly even "impatiently" so! However if this was the case, then where does being "relaxed" come into it? **The answer can only be this: <u>faith</u> is able to relax because it <u>trusts</u> the Word.** This can apply to us of course; if we trust in the creative power of God - we too can "relax" in faith - as we wait for His fulfilment!

As for the Holy Spirit, I prefer to see Him as being composed not tense - eager but restrained - until the Word had been spoken and He was "released" to perform it!

Let me add that the Holy Spirit is just as eager today as He was during the original creation. In fact God has never "stopped" creating and He wants to continue today through us - by His Word and His Spirit. Nothing about God has ever changed!

ONE GIVES LIFE
THE OTHER GIVES INSTRUCTION

This brings us to our main focal point. The Spirit gives life to the Word but the Spirit needs the "instruction" of the Word; without the Word He cannot create and without the Spirit the Word cannot literally come to pass.

Scripture repeatedly tells us that the **Spirit gives life** *(chiefly to the Word "in" us);* **"It is the Spirit who gives life [He is the Life-giver]...** The words *(truths)* that I have been speaking to you are spirit and life" *(John 6:63 AMPC)*. "...the letter killeth, but **the Spirit giveth life"** *(2 Corinthians 3:6)*. **"...the Spirit of life from God** entered into them..." *(Revelation 11:11)* "...he that soweth to the Spirit shall **of the Spirit reap life everlasting"** *(Galatians 6:8-9)*.

God spoke to me very clearly one day while studying this subject and said, **"There is no LIFE in the Word without the Spirit and no SUBSTANCE to the Spirit without the Word."** The Word became flesh and dwelt amongst us it said in John 1:14, and Jesus Himself *(the Word)* also needed this "life giving Spirit." We see this in the Authorised Version in 1 Corinthians 15:45 where it says, "The first man Adam was made a living soul; the last Adam *was made* a quickening spirit" or in the Amplified *(AMPC)* it is better said as, "...the last Adam *(Christ)* became a **life-giving Spirit** [restoring the dead to life]."

Remember if we are truly building His Kingdom, we become co-labourers of what He has "ordained." Then that which He brings to birth through us, we are also ordained to take-care of, nurture and protect, including all that He's revealed and intends to do through us *(we call this vision)*. For example, Adam was ordained to take care of the "garden," likewise we are ordained to take care of His Kingdom.

The Holy Spirit directed the Apostle Paul in all things. Before his conversion however, Paul lived by the religious word only, but after his conversion he lived by the Spirit and the Word.

A prophecy attributed to Smith Wigglesworth in 1947 states:

"During the next few decades there will be two distinct moves of the Holy Spirit across the church in Great Britain. The first move will affect every church that is open to receive it, and will be characterised by a restoration of the baptism and the gifts of the Holy Spirit. The second move of the Holy Spirit will result in people leaving historic churches and planting new churches. In the duration of each of these moves, the people who are involved will say, 'This is a great revival.' But the Lord says, 'No, neither is this the great revival but both are steps towards it.'"

"When the new church phase is on the wane, there will be evidence in the churches of something that has not been seen before: **a coming together of those with an emphasis on the word and those with an emphasis on the Spirit. When the Word and the Spirit come together, there will be the biggest move of the Holy Spirit that the nation, and indeed, the world has ever seen.**"

"It will mark the beginning of a revival that will eclipse anything that has been witnessed within these shores, even the Wesleyan and Welsh revivals of former years. The outpouring of God's Spirit will flow over from the United Kingdom to mainland Europe, and from there, will begin a missionary move to the ends of the earth."

THE RHEMA IS LIVING AND ACTIVE

As our opening scripture Hebrews 4:12 states, "the Word of God is living and active" in fact the Amplified *(AMPC)* does well again here by saying; **"...the Word that God speaks is alive and full of power [making it active, operative, energizing, and effective]"** whereas the Authorised only calls the Word of God, **"quick, and powerful..!"**

So it is clear then, that the Spirit gives life - He is the "life-giver." However He needs the Word *(Christ)* for "instruction" - otherwise He can only continue to "hover or brood" and this is never His purpose, intention or ultimate desire. Brooding is just a means to an end, not a means in itself. He is not content with just "being there." He always wants to be active - producing life because He is LIFE!

The Holy Spirit is never passive only composed! And He is only ever "inactive" when we make Him thus - especially when we fail to "speak" God's Word *(which He longs to bring to life)*. We must never fail to understand that whenever we "receive" a Word *(Rhema - God's Word)* that Word is "living and active" and is always looking to "manifest" itself - we must never abort, kill, stop, delay or hinder this divine course of action.

Finally, the very thing that God's Word "speaks" about - is what it is "intending-to-do" - such as healing. God speaks of healing because that is what He wants to DO *(manifest)*. I believe that the Holy Spirit still "broods" over people's lives today - for instance the sick and dying - He has to wait "longingly, lovingly and protectively" - unable to "act" until someone with living-faith comes to speak "life" over them; over their failing marriages, ministries or wayward children etc.

Speaking His Word - releases the power of that Word and as my wife always says when she teaches on intercession, "the Holy Spirit is always as willing as He is able," to fix any problem that we face. In fact 2 Peter 1:3 *(GW)* says, "His divine power has **given us everything we need for life..."**

The reality of this of course is that properly applied - broken lives can be restored and the dead can be raised! **By His stripes we are healed.** This spoken truth *(God's Word)* that is energized and given life to by the Spirit - has the power to bring this truth to pass/to birth/to manifestation. Only then are we truly "healed by His stripes" - this is God's "creative" Word in ACTION. Faith without action/works is always dead. In fact words that are not active are dead. **Even God's Word is inactive until it is spoken and the Spirit released to perform it.**

In closing: God's Word holds "highest" authority in the entire universe; the "highest-truth" and the "last word on everything" *(this must be true in our personal lives as well!)* This means that if we truly got-a-grip on God's Word for our lives - where it was truly "revelation" to us - then it would bring LIFE! Then we would truly begin to LIVE that Word. Yes!

Spirit and Word

Faith without works is dead - simply because if faith is not put to "work" it dies. We must "work" *(believe)* the Word of God otherwise it will always be "dead" to us. Ultimately, the Word only works for those who believe and then act upon it; LIVE it...! *(James 1:15; James 1:21; Matthew 26:41; 16:16; Deuteronomy 28:1; Luke 1:26-28)*

ENDNOTES:

1. Strong, James. S.T.D., L.L.D. 1890. Strong's Exhaustive Concordance, Dictionaries (Lexicon) of the Hebrew and Greek Words

2. This "Truth for the Journey" has been taken from: https://watchersofthe4kings.com

3. Unless otherwise indicated, all scripture references are taken from the King James Version of the Bible.

4. Scripture references marked AMPC are taken from the Amplified® Bible (AMPC), Copyright © 1954, 1958, 1962, 1964, 1965, 1987 by The Lockman Foundation. Used by permission. www.Lockman.org

5. Scripture references marked GW are taken from GOD'S WORD®, © 1995 God's Word to the Nations. Used by permission of Baker Publishing Group.

6. Scripture references marked NIV are taken from the HOLY BIBLE, NEW INTERNATIONAL VERSION ®. NIV ®. Copyright © 1973, 1978, 1984 by the International Bible Society. Used by permission of Zondervan Publishing House. All rights reserved.

Letter 27

Truth for the Journey

The Fellowship of the Holy Spirit

Letter to the Church, 1st October 2010

*T**he grace of the Lord Jesus Christ, and the love of God, and the fellowship of the Holy Spirit, [is] with you all! Amen.*

(2 Corinthians 13:14 YLT)

The last verse of 2 Corinthians is a powerful one and the Amplified Version *(AMPC)* says it like this: "The grace *(favor and spiritual blessing)* of the Lord Jesus Christ and the love of God and the **presence and fellowship** *(the communion and sharing together, and participation)* in the Holy Spirit be with you all. Amen *(so be it)*."

Everything in this verse points to a 3 fold companionship with God. Remembering that one of His names is also "Emmanuel," which means "God with us." This is reflected in the Young's Literal Translation above where it says "...the Holy Spirit [IS] with you all!"

All three Persons of the Godhead; Father, Son and Holy Spirit, are active in providing this companionship with us. Jesus brings grace and the Father brings love. Both, grace and love are so potent that they can only originate from God *(Ephesians 2:8; John 3:16)*. His grace allows us "entry" into divine companionship while His love "keeps" this companionship breathing and vibrant. However the Holy Spirit also plays a vital role in ensuring our companionship with the Almighty, and it is HIS "contribution" to this relationship that we focus on for today's Truth for the Journey: **"The fellowship of the Holy Spirit."**

We begin by looking into the Greek meaning for the word "fellowship" used in our opening scripture 2 Corinthians 13:14. This Greek word is "koinonia" that literally means: **communion, communication, contribution, distribution, joint participation, intimacy.** It could be said like this; **"communion by intimate participation!"** However it also involves words like *partnership, (social) intercourse* and *(pecuniary or economic) benefaction* - coming from the closely related words "koinonos" and "koinos" meaning *sharer, i.e. associate:* - companion, fellowship, partaker, partner *(see Strong's #G2844, #G2839)*.[1]

So as we can see this Greek word for "fellowship" *(koinonia)* is a complex, rich, and thoroughly fascinating

Greek approach to building community and teamwork. It has such a multitude of meanings that no single English word is adequate to express its depth and richness. Therefore when we look at this word, we can derive so much from it in order to help us decipher what is exactly meant or entailed by "fellowship" with the Holy Spirit. First of all let's break this up slightly for easier grasp - "koinonia" has three superb applications.

THE JOINT PARTICIPATION

The fellowship of the Holy Spirit is not a one-way street! It is a sharing of wills, feelings, and knowledge. We share what we have or know with Him and He shares what He has and knows with us! Jesus said, "He will tell you whatever He hears [from the Father; He will give the message that has been given to Him], and He will announce and declare to you the things that are to come [that will happen in the future]. He will honor and glorify Me because He will take of *(receive, draw upon)* what is Mine and will reveal *(declare, disclose, transmit)* it to you" *(John 16:13b-14 AMPC)*.

Just think, He knows the secrets of heaven and is willing to reveal those to whoever will "jointly participate" with Him. The Holy Spirit has direct access to the Father's heart, which means whatever the Father speaks; He hears and is able to communicate to us! In other words we can enjoy "inside information" if we will only "dare" to draw closer in fellowship with Him, as we are admonished to do in James 4:8; **"Draw nigh to God, and he will draw nigh to you."**

The original Greek here for "draw nigh" or "come close" depending on what translation of the bible you have -

literally means: "approach" or "be at hand" for Him. Once we "approach" God like this, or in other words "make ourselves available by being at hand" then God can reciprocate with His Presence! He approaches us in return and is always "at hand" for us! What an awesome reality this is. To have God Himself close by and always "at hand!" Can we fathom the beautiful implications of this and the impact that such fellowship can have on our everyday lives?

The only glitch or claw to this "drawing nigh" business of verse 8 of James chapter 4 is that we must "draw nigh" FIRST! Which quite plainly puts the overall "onus" onto us. The quality of the fellowship that we enjoy with God, or the regularity of such - largely rests with us and our willingness to "approach" Him or to be "at hand" for Him.

For sure "any" approach that we make towards God, could be seen only in terms of a "response" to what He has already "initiated" through Christ. For instance according to 1 John 4:19, "We love because he **first** loved us..." it was God who "initiated" love - not us! In fact we initiated nothing in this context. It came from and started with God. However in terms of **"relationship"** *(the two way street we are discussing here)*, our "willingness" is always a "prerequisite" and must always be evident *(to God and especially to ourselves!)*

As heaven's divine distributor the Holy Spirit equips and prepares us for the future. Through Him we can face any challenge that life throws at us! And within this type of "fellowship" we are able to communicate our intimate and most personal needs; whether desires of the heart or heart concerns; and is a type of fellowship that enjoys both "spontaneity and freedom" rather than dictatorial and dull monologue! In this respect we should always freely "welcome" the Holy Spirit into our lives; appreciating, respecting, adoring and fully recognizing Him in everything that we do.

THE APPLICATION OF A POTENT PARTNERSHIP

Secondly the type of fellowship that we are discussing here in this particular study - represents a most effective and potent partnership! All partnerships exist to enhance growth, productivity and profit. Partners strategize together and share in all successes and failures. However when we consider fellowship with the Holy Spirit in this way, **we must always recognise Him as the "Senior Partner"** *(simply because He brings so much more to the table than we do!)*

For example consider the infinite resources and knowledge that He possesses; which can only make His strategies and methods perfect and above reproach! In addition regard the fact that no matter how much He outranks everyone, He still leaves room for us to be heard every time! Nevertheless we do well to "allow" Him to strategize on our behalf - as He knows best and the results are always more consistent!

We must make ourselves available by always being "at hand" to fellowship with Him, so that He can communicate those strategies with us as He wants to do. We must always "live-ready" to listen to His instruction and be equally willing to receive His specialized help for the "follow-through" of that instruction! The best fact of all is that He not only lends us His expertise but also His "power!"

Remembering that even as partners who share victories - the credit must all be His! He is unable to fail and neither will we if we learn to follow and yield in the manner that we are discussing here. It is elementary then, that in the degree to which we "cooperate" is the degree to which we will experience success in and through our personal lives.

Everything the Holy Spirit does is to empower us. Therefore we can be certain that "fellowship" with Him, will only benefit our lives. Heaven's intentions can then be realized. It is through deep fellowship like this that History can be changed as a result! NOT sitting in a lotus position meditating and chanting in tongues - that is not "fellowship" - but a religious ritual that some might like to call "fellowship!" But true fellowship with the Holy Spirit is very much "active" and part of our everyday lives. He talks with us "on the go!" Nothing restricts Him. Not time or space! He is always ready and always willing for us to "plug in" and enjoy our "living-connection" with Him. In fact it should never be broken. We should not spend our Christian lives "travelling-in-and-out-of-His-presence" but learn to LIVE there!

In fact the kind of "fellowship" we discuss here is very active and accountable simply because the Holy Spirit specializes in transforming what is "written" instruction from the word of God into practical application in our lives. Therefore it is vital that we learn to partner with Him on every level; being open to His input and advice before making decisions.

I'm not suggesting that we need the Holy Spirit to tell us when to clean our teeth - some things we can work out for ourselves! When to wash and to eat etc.; and He gives us enough credit to do that sort of thing on our own! However when it comes to the larger decisions of life - it is a "learnt" discipline - to pass things with Him first. It takes time but we must pursue such a discipline - especially when the end product of living in such a way - has the potential to change other people's lives as a result.

Sensitivity to the Holy Spirit on this level means that He can depend on us to ACT in any given situation - no matter what the circumstances say. This is where we allow the "unction" of the Holy Spirit to dictate our thoughts rather than the conditions of the world around us.

In addition to that is the fact that our obedience has always a good influence on others, even if we cannot directly see the results of it with our own eyes - we can guarantee that if the Holy is in control - He always has others in mind and an agenda that pursues their freedom and liberty! **"Now the Lord is that Spirit: and where the Spirit of the Lord *is*, there *is* liberty"** *(2 Corinthians 3:17).*

It is important to add right now that the Holy Spirit does not just promote the "self-life" that the world does - rather He "demotes" selfishness and "promotes" selflessness! He is not our spiritual maid, who picks up the pieces that we leave behind or our PR who deals with all the "damage-control" in our lives - for all those mistakes we make! In fact because we live in a generation of "self-help" coaches and gurus - who make millions off the back of people who have no identity of their own - we could easily confuse the Holy Spirit with our own "personal-trainer" but I would like to suggest that He is SO MUCH MORE THAN THAT! It is a danger to limit the Holy Spirit to such "earthly" status!

On the other hand, He never "closes-shop" on us and is always available for us. He shares in our failures as much as our successes, so that the challenges of life don't overwhelm us. He moves in us, so that our spiritually-natural instincts are to "overcome" in situations rather than indulge in or enjoy "self-pity" too much!

In fact the world around us is obsessed with "self" - yet in Christ we learn that life is not all about "self" and we soon learn that we don't just exist to avoid or rescue ourselves from ourselves! Instead we learn to "overcome" in ways that help others as a result, and with His divine influence upon our lives, normal temptations should be more easily overcome.

In fact this is generally how we know if someone is truly walking with the Spirit of God or not - because if they really know Him *(and are known of Him)*, then the "conviction of Holiness" is always present. This means that they will not feel "well" with themselves, in the presence of sin and will conscientiously work on "adjusting" themselves; in pursuit of maturity and self control. Whereas those who are too comfortable around sin, are probably not walking too closely with the Holy Spirit at all!

For the sake of balance here and in the context of "evangelism" we cannot afford to be overly "delicate" about sin. It is then that we must be open to "embrace" those in the deepest sins - without becoming "one" with their sins in the process. For example Galatians 6:1 *(GW)* says this, "... if a person gets trapped by wrongdoing, those of you who are spiritual should help that person turn away from doing wrong. Do it in a gentle way. At the same time watch yourself so that you also are not tempted."

To continue however, with this application of "potent-partnership" - one of the greatest chapters in the bible that describes this privileged partnership we have with the Holy Spirit, is Romans 8. The entire chapter is a treasure in fact, but verse 26 just says, **"So too the [Holy] Spirit comes to our aid and bears us up in our weakness..."** *(AMPC)* What comfort this offers us. With the Holy Spirit "close at hand" like this, everything truly can "work together for good for those who love God" *(verse 28)*.

THE APPLICATION OF A UNITED MOVEMENT

This **third** and final application of "koinonia" is taken from another literal translation meaning; **"moving together with..."** We could say "travelling together with..!" As we know, the Holy Spirit excels in the area of "distribution," which can be seen in the context of our prayer lives. For instance He moves or travels with us "as" we pray, by "moving or transporting" our prayer from earth to heaven.

This is indicated in Romans 8:26. As usual the Amplified Version *(AMPC)* of the bible puts it more poignantly like this:

So too the [Holy] Spirit comes to our aid and bears us up in our weakness; for we do not know what prayer to offer nor how to offer it worthily as we ought, but the Spirit

*Himself **goes to meet** our supplication and pleads in our behalf with unspeakable yearnings and groanings too deep for utterance.*

So with all this in mind, when it next becomes time for the "Grace" to be declared over the people at the end of a meeting - we must all say it with much more "conviction" because now we possess a better grasp on its original meaning *(2 Corinthians 13:14)*. Fellowship *(koinonia)* is our greatest life's honour - because it represents a living "companionship, intimacy and working together with" Almighty God. We must never forget that "KNOWING HIM - IS LOVING HIM" and we must always thank Him for the GRACE, LOVE AND FELLOWSHIP that He has placed in our lives. Hallelujah!

ENDNOTES:

1. Strong, James. S.T.D., L.L.D. 1890. Strong's Exhaustive Concordance, Dictionaries (Lexicon) of the Hebrew and Greek Words

2. This "Truth for the Journey" has been taken from: https://watchersofthe4kings.com

3. Unless otherwise indicated, all scripture references are taken from the King James Version of the Bible.

4. Scripture references marked AMPC are taken from the Amplified® Bible (AMPC), Copyright © 1954, 1958, 1962, 1964, 1965, 1987 by The Lockman Foundation. Used by permission. www.Lockman.org

5. Scripture references marked GW are taken from GOD'S WORD®, © 1995 God's Word to the Nations. Used by permission of Baker Publishing Group.

6. Scripture quotations marked YLT are taken from the Young's Literal Translation of the bible.

Letter 28

Truth for the Journey

Cultivating a Deep and Daily Fellowship with the Holy Spirit

Letter to the Church, 5th October 2010

*If you have any encouragement from being united with Christ, if any comfort from his love, if any **fellowship with the Spirit**, if any tenderness and compassion, then make my joy complete by being like-minded, having the same love, being one in spirit and purpose.*
(Philippians 2:1-2 NIV)

Have you ever yearned for a deeper walk with the Holy Spirit? I know that I have, and often desire to go deeper still. I have enjoyed these refreshing articles on the Holy Spirit myself. With feedback already coming in, I know that you have been enjoying them also that's why I have included them in this book. So continue with me in these successive studies on the Holy Spirit and I trust that revelation and inspiration will flood your heart and trigger a level of fellowship with the Holy Spirit that you never previously thought possible!

As we have already found out, this Greek word *koinōnia* (κοινωνία *Strong's #G2842)*[1] which is continually used in the New Testament for **"fellowship"** has many applications. We can refer to last Truth for the Journey for a recap, but let's move on to the Vine's Expository Dictionary where the words given to describe *koinōnia* are as follows: *communicate (-tion), communion, contribution, and fellowship.*[2] From this we can see that a major part of fellowship is just straightforward **"communication;"** something that we must learn to do adequately with the Holy Spirit on a daily basis.

Again it is a learning process, just as a married couple "never" cease to learn of new and better ways to "communicate" with each other. As the individual grows and their understanding expands, so can the quality of the fellowship involved. In fact fellowship can be a deeply enriching experience that many miss out on, not only in their everyday relationships, but chiefly with the Holy Spirit.

If we would learn better how to communicate, not only would this benefit us, but all those inside our circle of influence. When communication breaks-down, so do the relationships involved; therefore on all fronts must we guard against such break-downs and pursue better methods of communication - but all this is just on a human level.

Now however, let's continue with our subject of "fellowship with the Holy Spirit" as mentioned in our opening scripture. We can use this in two different contexts, as do the different translations of the bible;

1. Fellowship "shared" with other believers "in" the Spirit.
2. Fellowship "directly-with" the Holy Spirit.

For example the NIV of our opening scripture states; **"if any fellowship with the Spirit"** whereas the Authorised Version states, "if any fellowship **of** the Spirit..." and the Amplified version *(AMPC)* says; "by whatever **participation** in the [Holy] Spirit **[we share]**."

So you see the different emphasis that is covered. I prefer the NIV in this instance; as we are currently emphasising on fellowship "with" the Holy Spirit, as the third "person" of the Trinity. It is therefore accurate to say that - "fellowship with the Holy Spirit" - is a blessing for "all" believers in Christ to enjoy *(as already seen in 2 Corinthians 13:14 and Philippians 2:1)*.

Remembering that we are "sealed" with the Holy Spirit of promise *(Ephesians 1:13, for salvation)* and then "baptized" with the Spirit *(Matthew 3:11, Mark 1:8; Acts 2:2-4 - receive an infilling)*. One places us in the Body and the other empowers us for works of service.

WE MUST ABIDE IN CHRIST

To continue; the only thing that can mar this divine fellowship with the Holy Spirit is "un-confessed sin." Only as we "abide" in Christ and His finished work of the cross - can we "abide" in communion *(union)* with His Spirit. Therefore when it comes to "sin" we can have confidence that when, "... we confess our sins, He is faithful and righteous to forgive us our sins and to cleanse us from all unrighteousness" *(1 John 1:9 NASB)*. This makes fellowship with the Holy Spirit so vital because we are united to Christ in the bonds of the Holy Spirit.

Our fellowship with the Spirit is of utmost importance because **"He seeks partnership with us..."** in life and in ministry. His resources are unlimited, inexhaustible, and His power is invincible. We might long for intimate fellowship with Him, but it is absolutely true that, **"He longs for and regularly pursues intimate fellowship with us."** He longs to be admitted to the inner life of our souls. Again I use this emphasis that **"He"** seeks and pursues partnership and fellowship with us, because He knows better than we, that without His partnership and close fellowship; that those things which He has specifically called us to do *(on this earth)* will go "unachieved."

It has been said that the wealthiest place on earth is the "Graveyard!" There are many dreams, business ventures and so forth that have gone there unfulfilled. The Holy Spirit however, if allowed, to steer and direct us - will achieve heaven's mandates in and through our lives. Therefore, true fulfilment can only come via Him! This speaks of PURPOSE - and there is certainly much purpose to this fellowship with the Holy Spirit.

For instance it is not idle past-time, which simply enjoys each other's presence - like young lovers! In fact this often makes me feel so uncomfortable, when I hear people, especially women *(of all ages),* speak of their relationship with God, as if in a romantic way. Personally I believe that they have bought into a deception.

Our relationship with God, as a whole, can never be estimated in this way. It is erroneous and underlines the attempt that people often make, when they try to see God *(who is "infinite")* in a "finite" way. In other words, we cannot ever measure God on mere human levels or standards.

There is nothing "sexual" about our relationship with Him, albeit that we often use the word "intimacy" - however this is in context with a "heart-condition" and not something to be confused with "romantic-notions." Women especially have to be careful with this. Some men do this also of course, but are generally less inclined to go down that route of thinking.

DON'T ALLOW THE WORLD TO DETRACT

However to continue with this thought of what hinders our "fellowship or union" with the Spirit, let me suggest that there are "many" things such as; attitudes, reservations, interests, disbeliefs, prayerlessness, selfish-ambitions, arrogant pride, anger, bitterness, and many more that grieve and quench His work.

This is why we must cultivate our lives; so that we can "remain" in fellowship with Him. This involves as much willing "self-adjustment" as possible! Of course He never leaves or forsakes us, but we are discussing the subject of fellowship here. To illustrate this better; one day in my personal prayer time, I said to God, **"Father don't take Your Holy Spirit from me."** His swift reply to me was simply this, **"Don't leave my presence then..!"** That pretty much speaks for itself!

Still we must emphasize on this fact that there is PURPOSE to everything in God, just like Romans 8:28 says, "...to them who are the called according to *his* purpose" *(KJV)*. There is certainly plenty of divine PURPOSE in our daily union with the Holy Spirit. If such was not the case - then perhaps God would have us in heaven already by now! But as we know, there is still much work to be done. Some folks imagine that fellowship with God is just some "dreamy" type of meditation! But in actual fact there remains a very "active" purpose to our "fellowship" with God.

In addition, let me point out that when our lives line up "in agreement" with the Holy Spirit - our personalities becomes "quickened" and "sanctified" and our desire is to be in "constant" fellowship with Him. This is where we get our "recharge;" where we soak up heaven's resources to make our lives effective.

This is echoed and reflected by Isaiah in chapter 40 where he states,

> *Even youths grow tired and weary, and young men stumble and fall; but those who hope in the LORD will* **renew their strength.** *They will soar on wings like*

eagles; they will run and not grow weary, they will walk and not be faint.

(Isaiah 40:30-31 NIV)

This "renewing" of strength actually refers to an "exchange" of strength. How awesome this is! During our fellowship with Him, we actually exchange our own "limited" human strength and resources for His! There is no comparison with this and the joy of fellowship on this level comes only through Christ and His finished work of the cross.

Now as a consequence, today and everyday God makes Himself continually available for us to enjoy fellowship with Him like this. Each and every believer is sanctioned *(authorized by Christ)* to enjoy such a rich and glorious companionship with His Spirit. Hallelujah!

TAKE A DAY AT A TIME

When we learn to cooperate with Him, He comes to give us a daily life that overflows with the fruit of the Spirit. When we are in agreement with Him - His power operates in and through us. Ministry becomes a daily adventure with Him at the helm. Our empathy for the needy is deepened and enlightened. Our compassion for the lost soul is strengthened and our prayer lives invigorated. Ordinary Christians become empowered when clothed with the Spirit of God.

This fellowship, joint-participation, partnership and communion, with the Holy Spirit - is communion with the

LORD God. It **should** affect everything we do in our Christian life and ministry - we must never neglect such sweet and potent fellowship with the Holy Spirit. In fact as Christians, we're "called" to fellowship with the Holy Spirit. It's not in fact an "option!" *(Just for the crazy Pentecostals or Holy Rollers!)* Furthermore for some folks, all they know about the Holy Spirit is that He's the one who makes them speak in other tongues. However, there's more to the Person and ministry of the Holy Spirit than this. We are called to fellowship with Him **every day** and it is then that we discover exactly what He's come to do in our lives.

The Lord Jesus said "...the Comforter *(Counselor, Helper, Intercessor, Advocate, Strengthener, Standby)*, the Holy Spirit, Whom the Father will send in My name [in My place, to represent Me and act on My behalf], He will teach you all things. And He will cause you to recall *(will remind you of, bring to your remembrance)* everything I have told you" *(John 14:26 AMPC)*. This reveals the benefits and blessings of daily fellowship with the Holy Spirit in our lives: He'll teach, counsel, help, defend, strengthen and always be there as our standby when we need Him and when our natural strength fails us!

Finally the Holy Spirit is not fire, smoke, wind or a dove; He's a real person. He's the secret of my life. He talks with me and I talk with Him! He shows me what to do, when to do it and how to do it. I can never be confused about anything because the Holy Spirit guides me. He's not a "spirit-guide" as the world calls it. No! He is *THE Guide!* Once any of us learn to fellowship with the Holy Spirit each day like this, we then learn to hear His voice as we yield - spirit, soul and body - to Him.

Only then will we truly let Him work, talk and function through us. **He wants us to enjoy rich fellowship with Him every single day.**

ENDNOTES:

1. Strong, James. S.T.D., L.L.D. 1890. Strong's Exhaustive Concordance, Dictionaries (Lexicon) of the Hebrew and Greek Words

2. Vine's Expository Dictionary of New Testament Words, by W.E. VINE, Printed by Lowe & Brydone Printers Ltd, Thetford, Norfolk

3. This "Truth for the Journey" has been taken from: https://watchersofthe4kings.com

4. Scripture references marked AMPC are taken from the Amplified® Bible (AMPC), Copyright © 1954, 1958, 1962, 1964, 1965, 1987 by The Lockman Foundation. Used by permission. www.Lockman.org

5. Scripture references marked KJV are taken from the King James Version of the Bible.

6. Scripture marked NASB are taken from the New American Standard Bible®, Copyright © 1960, 1962, 1963, 1968, 1971, 1972, 1973, 1975, 1977, 1995 by The Lockman Foundation. Used by permission.

7. Scripture references marked NIV are taken from the HOLY BIBLE, NEW INTERNATIONAL VERSION ®. NIV ®. Copyright © 1973, 1978, 1984 by the International Bible Society. Used by permission of Zondervan Publishing House. All rights reserved.

Letter 29

Truth for the Journey

Biblical Mandate for Fellowship with God's Spirit

Letter to the Church, 9th October 2010

*When the **Friend** comes, the Spirit of the Truth, he will take you by the hand and guide you into all the truth there is. **He** won't draw attention to **himself**, but will make sense out of what is about to happen and, indeed, out of all that I have done and said. **He** will honor me; **he** will take from me and deliver it to you...*

(John 16:13 MSG)

During the last study we looked at "Cultivating a deep and *daily* fellowship with the Holy Spirit" and we will start where we left off, knowing that when it comes to fellowship with Him, it is vitally important to have a firm understanding of just whom we are relating to. He is not a mystical being for instance, but a distinct person, namely the third person of the trinity.

As we go deeper now let's look at what the Spirit does - this will aid us in our grasp of who He really is and how we can relate to Him in our everyday lives. I have continually mentioned, "everyday" or "daily" throughout these studies, simply because our fellowship with the Holy Spirit is something that we should pursue daily.

Actually there is much about the Lord in scripture that is "daily" such as; "daily bread," *(Matthew 6:11)* "fresh manna every morning" *(Exodus 16:21)*, "mercy is new every day" *(Lamentations 3:22-23)* "take up our cross daily" *(Luke 9:23)* and so forth. Why? Because when something is "living" it is always a "daily experience."

KEEPING IT DAILY HELPS KEEPING IT FRESH!

Bread is predominantly associated with scripture and is something, which for the most part, goes particularly stale after just one day! Same too concerning our relationship with the Holy Spirit, we must keep it fresh. In fact everything about our relationship with God must be kept fresh - not stale, stuffy or religious! We achieve this by approaching Him and welcoming Him afresh - every single day.

This daily pursuit is a journey of discovery that changes our personality in the process. So why don't more people in general try it, what is their cramp? One obvious hurdle that folks have grappled with is the fact that unlike Jesus *(who we saw dwelt amongst us)*, people can't see the Spirit of God with "flesh and bones" *(John 1:14; Luke 24:39)*. This single difficulty throughout church history has led some to either ignore the Spirit completely in their day-to-day Christian lives or keep Him as some kind of spiritual "spare tire" for emergencies only.

However it is only a sheer lack of understanding that can be the culprit here, for such neglect of this significant member of the Trinity. For example scripture certifies that we are born of the Spirit *(John 3:6)* and that our bodies are the temple of the Holy Spirit - who indwells us, *(Romans 8:9, 11, 14-16)* and that His witness gives us assurance that we are children of God. Also as mentioned in the previous Truth for the Journey, we are baptized by one Spirit into the body of Christ and we have access to God by the same Spirit *(1 Corinthians 12:13; Ephesians 2:14)*.

With all this in mind - who would willingly dare to be so casual or cavalier in their attitude towards the Holy Spirit? Ignorance can be the only cause; including deception and false teaching that has always dogged and hindered believers in their perception of Him. Our adversary works over time to ensure this "dull perception" knowing better than we just how "potent" we would be if fully surrendered to the Holy Spirit.

There is a huge difference throughout church history between Christians who walked with the Holy Spirit and those who didn't - quite simply they lacked essential power! Still today we have a choice whether to be "thrilled, filled, or spilled." In other words, mere "excitement" *(being thrilled)* counts for nothing compared to being fully "surrendered" *(filled)* and "used" *(spilled)* by Him!

Nevertheless those who struggle to know the Holy Spirit personally are chiefly those who struggle to see Him as a "personality." It is usually the religious folks who have the most difficulty with this!

A definition of "personality" *(on a human level at least)* refers in general to a complexity of attributes such as: behavioural, temperamental, emotional and mental - that help characterize the uniqueness of an individual. Whereas a more simple definition of "personality" refers to "person-like-qualities," such as: the ability to talk and to listen *(a.k.a. "the ability to communicate")* to think and to reason; to feel and to have emotions; decision making and free will.

PERSONALITY UNMISTAKABLY VERIFIED

When broken down like this - especially in reference to the Holy Spirit - it becomes abundantly clear that He does indeed have a "person-ality" - that of which is unmistakably verified throughout scripture.

For example: Jesus and Paul both continually referred to the Holy Spirit as "He," not "It" *(John 14:16, 17, 26; 15:26; 16:7, 8, 13, 14)*. Then our opening scripture refers continually to His "personage" John 16:13-14; "Howbeit when **He,** the Spirit of truth, is come, **He** will guide you into all truth: for **He** shall not speak of **Himself**; but whatsoever **He** shall hear, that shall **He** speak: and **He** will show you things to come.

He shall glorify Me..." Luke 2:26 sees Him "speaking" to man, "...it was revealed unto him by the Holy Ghost" and in various scriptures from both Old and New Testaments, specific qualities of His character are well pointed out; **Goodness:** *(Nehemiah 9:20; Galatians 5:22, 23).* **Holiness:** *(Romans 1:4).* **Truth:** *(John 14:17; 15:26; 16:13).* **Grace:** *(Hebrews 10:29; Zechariah 12:10).* **Comfort:** *(John 14:26; 15:26).* **Patience, love, gentleness,** etc.: *(Galatians 5:22, 23).*

Most significantly the Holy Spirit is "one with God" *(Isaiah 48:16; Matthew 28:19; Acts 5:3, 4; 1 Corinthians 3:16; 6:19; 12:4-6; 2 Corinthians 13:14; 1 John 5:7).* Therefore He has all the attributes of God - He is eternal *(Hebrews 9:14).* He was present with God in the creation of the world - *(Genesis 1:2, 3; Job 26:13; 33:4; Psalms 104:30).* He is "omnipresent" *(Psalms 139:7-10).* He is "omniscient" *(Isaiah 40:13; 1 Corinthians 2:10, 11).* He is "omnipotent" *(Psalms 104:30).*

Yet He is a distinct personality, apart from both the Father and the Son, besides that scripture uses many types of symbols to describe His many functions and responsibilities, including many Old Testament scriptures that identify Him *(Isaiah 11:2; 42:1; 48:16; 61:1; 63:9; Ezekiel 36:26, 27).* So as far as scripture is concerned the Holy Spirit is undeniably a "personality" and a very powerful one at that!

THE CRUX OF THE PROBLEM

Consequently those who lack revelation of God's Word will be the ones who struggle to relate to Him. They will posses limited perception of who the Spirit of God is; for example an impersonal "power" or "force" such as electricity! This impersonal view of Him is the crux of their problem. And while there are "mystical" and "ancient philosophies" that present a plethora of "counterfeit-personalities" for folks to "relate to" - they are no more than cleverly designed plans that appeal to the "spiritual curiosity" of millions who are completely distracted and beguiled from the real McCoy.

Every believer however must eliminate "any" obstacle that hinders their fellowship with the Holy Spirit and not be duped by religious doctrines or the infiltration of worldly philosophies - which are equally misleading! For instance it could be said that mainline evangelical Christianity has no problem with the doctrine of the Trinity but their challenge comes with this issue of relating to the Holy Spirit on a "personal" level. Until this is resolved, fellowship with Him will always be disputed; meaning that many will fail to give Him the place that He truly deserves. The Word and the Holy Spirit must be working in conjunction in our lives, without which we have no revelation and our endeavours will be Godless!

To continue both Old and New Testaments report the work of the Spirit extensively. "This is the word of the LORD to Zerubbabel: 'Not by might nor by power, but by My Spirit,' Says the LORD of hosts" *(Zechariah 4:6 NKJV)*.

> *I will pour out My Spirit on all flesh; your sons and your daughters shall prophesy, your old men shall dream dreams, your young men shall see visions. And also on my menservants and on My maidservants I will pour out My Spirit in those days.*
> *(Joel 2:28-29 NKJV)*

Jesus was anointed with the Holy Spirit *(Acts 10:38)* and led by the Spirit to be tempted by Satan and returning in the power of the Spirit *(Luke 4:1-2, 14)*. Jesus cast out evil spirits by the Holy Spirit *(Matthew 12:28)*.

In fact, it would not be incorrect to suggest that the entire ministry of our Lord, was influenced by and "one" with the anointing of the Holy Spirit. Jesus Himself qualified this by saying,

> *The Spirit of the Lord is upon me, because he hath anointed me to preach the gospel to the poor; he hath sent me to heal the broken hearted, to preach deliverance to the captives, and recovering of sight to the blind, to set at liberty them that are bruised, To preach the acceptable year of the Lord.*
> *(Luke 4:18-19)*

Once we master this continual fellowship with the Holy Spirit, as believers we will also enjoy the intimate bond of fellowship which binds us together in Christ. There is also fellowship with the Father and the Son as seen here in 1 John 1:3 *(AMPC)*; "What we have seen and [ourselves] heard, we are also telling you, so that you too may realize and enjoy fellowship as partners and partakers with us. And [this] fellowship that we have [which is a distinguishing mark of Christians] is with the Father and with His Son Jesus Christ *(the Messiah).*"

Then also in 1 Corinthians 1:9 *(AMPC)* it speaks of specific fellowship with the Son; "God is faithful *(reliable, trustworthy, and therefore ever true to His promise, and He can be depended on)*; by Him you were called into companionship and participation with His Son, Jesus Christ our Lord."

ONE YET THREE

However as ONE yet THREE - Father, Son and Spirit - remain very distinct personalities. Even though our fellowship is with all of them our emphasis remains the Holy Spirit and the following list of sins that are directly hostile to the person and ministry of the Holy Spirit, must be avoided by anyone seeking to cultivate a genuine fellowship with Him.

> **Grieving Him:** *(Ephesians 4:30)* by adopting behaviour contrary to the fruits; bitterness, unforgiveness, etc.
> **Quenching Him:** *(1 Thessalonians 5:19)* by disallowing the gifts and anointing to work through our lives.
> **Insulting Him:** *(Hebrews 10:29)* through deliberate sin even after receiving knowledge of truth.
> **Resisting Him:** *(Acts 7:51)* going in the opposite direction to the definite guidance of the Spirit.
> **Vexing Him:** *(Isaiah 63:10)* through intentional rebellion against His leadership.
> **Lying to Him:** *(Acts 5:3)* by speaking untruths to His anointed men and women in order to deceive.
> **Testing Him:** *(Acts 5:9)* by provoking Him into action - not out of faith but out of fear.
> **Blaspheming Him:** *(Matthew 12:31, 32)* by attributing the things of Him to demons.
> **Striving with Him:** *(Genesis 6:3)* by walking in the flesh continually against His promptings.
> **Rebelling against Him:** *(Psalms 106:33)* by refusing His instructions.

As believers our lives are supernatural. Our fallen natures continue to rage against us *(Galatians 5:16; Romans 7:14-22)* and therefore we continually need to be empowered from within and above in order to live and walk worthy of our calling. Our Lord explained that the Spirit will guide us into all truth and give us ability to cope with life and its stresses. With a cultivated lifestyle that is one with Him, we can avoid doctrinal pitfalls and the trickery of our adversary by trusting our "Paraclete" to outwit him *(1 Peter 5:8; John 16:12-13)*.

Sensitivity comes via spending time in His presence and is the only way that we can gain firsthand knowledge and gain the skills of detection that we need concerning what grieves and pleases him moment by moment. Gradually we experience growth in all these areas, the awkwardness flees and a fluent relationship emerges with maturity.

Finally possibly most importantly, as we have an "abandoned devotion" towards God's Word - devouring scripture and making it the final word on every issue - also means that we will always respect the authority of the Spirit who never speaks or gives instruction contrary to the Word. All in all we eventually find ourselves enjoying His company above all else which finally determines that we have cultivated such a passion for Him, that counts the passions of this world as dung! *(Philippians 3:8)*

ENDNOTES:

1. This "Truth for the Journey" has been taken from: https://watchersofthe4kings.com

2. Unless otherwise indicated, all scripture references are taken from the King James Version of the Bible.

3. Scripture references marked AMPC are taken from the Amplified® Bible (AMPC), Copyright © 1954, 1958, 1962, 1964, 1965, 1987 by The Lockman Foundation. Used by permission. www.Lockman.org

4. Scripture quotations marked MSG are taken from The Message. Copyright © 1993, 1994, 1995, 1996, 2000, 2001, 2002. Used by permission of NavPress Publishing Group.

5. Scripture references marked NKJV are taken from the New King James Version. Copyright © 1982 by Thomas Nelson, 1982 by Thomas Nelson, Inc. Used by permission. All rights reserved.

Letter 30

Truth for the Journey

Can We Talk to the Holy Spirit and Hear His Voice

Letter to the Church, 13th October 2010

*However, I am telling you nothing but the truth when I say it is profitable (good, expedient, advantageous) for you that I go away. Because if I do not go away, the Comforter (Counselor, Helper, Advocate, Intercessor, Strengthener, Standby) will not come to you [into close fellowship with you]; **but if I go away, I will send Him to you [to be in close fellowship with you]**.*

(John 16:7 AMPC)

Communicating with the Holy Spirit, Hearing His voice and responding to it has been the cause of much "theological headache" in every generation! Have you ever wondered "can I talk to the Holy Spirit?" or "Am I allowed to speak back to Him if He talks to me?" Again, this may seem elementary for some, but stuff of nightmares for others!

Some may ask do we only pray to the Father in the name of the Son, or do we ignore the Father completely and only communicate with the Son? How do we focus on all three of the Trinity and yet maintain an intimate relationship with all three? What is God's truest intention for our relationship with Him - singular and plural? How do we view it and how do we have proper success with it; knowing that everything hinges on our right relations with God?

Therefore as we continue with this focus on the Holy Spirit and in particular our relationship with Him, let us consider the words Jesus spoke as He ascended to heaven. This included the Holy Spirit, and was in effect His last given instructions while still in the flesh on this earth: "But ye shall receive power, after that the Holy Ghost is come upon you: and ye shall be witnesses unto me both in Jerusalem, and in all Judaea, and in Samaria, and unto the uttermost part of the earth. And when he had spoken these things, while they beheld, he was taken up; and a cloud received him out of their sight" *(Acts 1:8-9 KJV)*.

So His parting words to His disciples were expressly about their future dealings with none other than the Holy Spirit. This goes hand in glove with what Jesus said prior to that in John 16:

However, I am telling you nothing but the truth when I say it is profitable (good, expedient, advantageous) for you

> *that I go away. Because if I do not go away, the Comforter (Counsellor, Helper, Advocate, Intercessor, Strengthener, Standby) will not come to you [into close fellowship with you]; but if I go away, I will send Him to you [to be in close fellowship with you].*
>
> (John 16:7 AMPC)

To be in "close fellowship" as the amplified version states it, this must involve close "communication." If we want to get technical, it is also the exchanging of or the transmission of messages! As my wife often says, meditating, practicing the presence and fellowshipping with the Holy Spirit is not akin to contemplating our navels or doing yoga! It is a place of genuine exchange. Exchange of strength *(Isaiah 40:31)* of ideas, thoughts, impressions, revelation, teaching, desires etc... In fact so much can come out of it. Time spent with the Holy Spirit can be so rich.

NOT ENTERTAINING BUT ENRICHING

I use that word "entertainment" because we are becoming so schooled in all-things-entertainment, that we have lost the art of just sitting "still." It is all a ploy. If our minds are so full, of celebrity gossip that we are unable to be still and know that He is God, then we have lost the plot altogether!

It is a discipline to sit in the presence of God. To stay there long enough to know Him in reality; to appreciate Him; to lend our minds to Him - in other words to hold our thoughts long enough and our concentration long enough to give Him the quality of time and focus that He alone deserves. First place is first place. He should not have to "compete" for our time, our thoughts, or our exchange. It should readily be given to Him. In a humble expression of love, trust, union, and friendship; all of which is the essence of "relationship."

We must exercise wisdom of course, plus we must remain open to the genuine manifestations of the Spirit and not allow the weird and wacky to "shut us down." Plus all things of the Spirit cut "crosswise" with the things of the carnal mind anyway, as we see here in Romans 8:7 *(AMPC)* "... the mind of the flesh [with its carnal thoughts and purposes] is hostile to God, for it does not submit itself to God's Law; indeed it cannot." Therefore we must never look for acceptance from others when dealing with the things of the Spirit. Instead we must always keep our eyes on Christ and His Word to keep things pure and accurate.

THE POWER OF GOD'S TOUCH

When folks shake - and I have seen this a lot over the years, this is just the power of God touching "earthen vessels!" Shaking is just a power encounter. And some folks are more open to this than others - but they are not more special. All of us must learn to yield more to His presence and allow our vessels to be filled up regularly. For some, the mere "filling of their vessel" creates manifestations. Some of these manifestations are demonic simply because they scramble to get out of the way! However there are some signs we can look for that show when the Spirit of God is resting on someone or whether it is demonic.

We will look at these just quickly here. **But a word of warning** - signs can lie - so we must not be directed by them, they are just an aid. For instance glittering on people's faces with a slight sweat; heat, eye lids fluttering, are all signs we can look for when someone is being touched by the Holy Spirit. Whereas eyes rolling backwards and stiffness - can all be signs of demonic manifestation. However pain can sometimes be a word of knowledge to indicate that someone needs a healing. Also we can sometimes "see" things; such as text running across our minds *(i.e. scripture),* or we can have just a "knowing" about things, as we are meant to be "one" with the Lord. However it is not all about feelings.

Finally - and there is so much to this subject that it cannot be exhausted here but provide some pointers. However to close on our original question, "When He talks to us, can we talk back?" the answer has to be "yes of course!" Others will ask "Can we be led by the Spirit or only by the Word?" For this I believe that scripture is clear that we must be led by the Spirit, although He never acts independently of the Word - in fact the whole God-head never works separately.

Throughout scripture we see them "working together" and one example of this is when Jesus was baptised in the river Jordan; all three were mentioned as being present; Father, Son and Holy Spirit *(Matthew 3:16-17).* Secondly when Jesus spoke His final words to His disciples all three are mentioned inseparable again, "All authority in heaven and on earth has been given to me. So wherever you go, make disciples of all nations: Baptize them in the name of the **Father, and of the Son, and of the Holy Spirit"** *(Matthew 28:18-19 GW).*

ERROR CAN BE AVOIDED

This means that any error can be avoided by remembering that they work in conjunction with each other and never apart. If we feel directed to do something that is against scripture - then we can be certain that it is not the Holy Spirit directing us, but some "other" spirit. In fact any time we doubt the leading of the Spirit, all we have to do is line it up to the Word, once we can see it there in the Word, we can then have *"peace"* to move out on it - accepting it as the genuine leading of the Spirit.

A strong indication that all is well is the peace of God as seen here in Colossians 3:15 of the Amplified version *(AMPC)*, "And **let the peace** *(soul harmony which comes)* from Christ **rule** *(act as umpire continually)* **in your hearts [deciding and settling with finality all questions that arise in your minds..."** *(See also Philippians 4:7 and Romans 14:17).* Scripture promises that He leads us into all truth and will guide us; "Howbeit when he, the Spirit of truth, is come, **he will guide you into all truth:** for he shall not **speak** of himself; but whatsoever he shall hear, [that] shall he **speak:** and he will **shew** you things to come" *(John 16:13 KJV).*

Evidently then the Holy Spirit does "speak"- but it is "what" He speaks that is of the most importance. He speaks "truth" and this is the only distinguishing line that we have where the Holy Spirit is concerned. He speaks truth and nothing else. That is how we know it is Him and not some other spirit. A good reason also to really KNOW the Word! Too many people are easily deceived; we must not be one of them. Particularly like those who get into spiritual things without God's Spirit or Word - which is only spiritualism - but not Christianity.

Paul the apostle encountered on Mars Hill in Greece, the "great thinkers" of their day. Even today with "information overload" we also have folks who know everything and know nothing! And as those Paul encountered back then - who were willing to "hear-anything" - but not willing to "believe-anything" - the same is true of our generation *(see 1 Timothy 4:1).*

People want a spiritualism that they can encounter but still be in control of. But those who walk by the Spirit of God - have given up control. They are governed by the Father, Son and Holy Spirit together and when you meet someone who is genuinely governed by God like this - with the Holy Spirit at the helm - it is never easy to forget meeting this kind of person "And they... yet shall they know and realize that there has been a prophet among them" *(Ezekiel 2:5 AMPC).*

ENDNOTES:

1. This "Truth for the Journey" has been taken from: https://watchersofthe4kings.com

2. Scripture references marked AMPC are taken from the Amplified® Bible (AMPC), Copyright © 1954, 1958, 1962, 1964, 1965, 1987 by The Lockman Foundation. Used by permission. www.Lockman.org

3. Scripture references marked GW are taken from GOD'S WORD®, © 1995 God's Word to the Nations. Used by permission of Baker Publishing Group.

4. Scripture references marked KJV are taken from the King James Version of the Bible.

Letter 31

Truth for the Journey

Experience vs. Truth

Letter to the Church, 15th October 2010

The Spirit-filled walk demands... that we live in the Word of God as a fish lives in the sea.
(A.W. Tozer)

We need to look at the reality of experience verses truth. **Do we give too much leverage to the experience and too little to truth?** Are we out of balance and do we seek maturity in all things spiritual or are we content to be spiritual novices forever?

To get to a place of maturity we have to start off from a place of immaturity. And there is room for all of us to learn. There are many different ways of hearing the voice of

God's Spirit along with different ways to feel His presence. Although it's not necessary to "feel" anything, especially when it comes to obedience - we must "step out" and let the feelings catch us up! Each morning we can wake up saying, "Thank You God that You are here. Wherever I am You are there. In fact there is no place that I could be - that You are not!"

In other words we can be totally sure and "convinced" of the presence of God, regardless of whether we "feel" anything or not! In fact if we never "feel" anything... it changes nothing. He is always there! On the other hand it is still important to practice the presence of God, learning to be sensitive; knowing when and how to yield.

The Holy Spirit is always "one" with the Word of God, and will never violate its clear boundaries. This is the only way that we can expose the counterfeit. If the experience doesn't line up with God's Word, then it does not line up with God's Spirit either. It is really that simple and we must endeavour to rightly divide the Word so that our private-interpretation doesn't line up with the counterfeit instead! Some folks spend most of their time trying to get the Word of God to say what they are saying rather than prayerfully studying it and allowing the Holy Spirit to show it to them by divine "revelation." He is our teacher and leads us into all truth.

Technically we could say that He is obedient to His own Word, in the context that He won't violate its conditions any more than He expects us not to. So to uncover the counterfeit manifestations of the Spirit we need to know His Word.

Then we can be sure of what He would "not" do as much as what He "would" do in any given situation; while always remaining open to learn new things. The Holy Spirit for instance is not always predictable and there will always be new things to find out about Him!

DISCERNMENT NOT SUSPICION

We do need however "discernment," not "suspicion" but real discernment; as the scripture calls it, the ability *(gift)* to distinguish between spirits; "To another the working of miracles, to another prophetic insight *(the gift of interpreting the divine will and purpose)*; **to another the ability to discern and distinguish between [the utterances of true] spirits [and false ones],** to another various kinds of [unknown] tongues, to another the ability to interpret [such] tongues..." *(1 Corinthians 12:10 AMPC)*

Another translation simply says, "...can tell the difference between spirits" *(GW)*. Therefore operating with the Spirit of God is not all about the "feel good factor" - rather it is all about lining things up with His Word.

The Holy Spirit stirs things up - including us! Therefore some manifestations are caused. Not everything that we assume is the Holy Spirit - is actually the Holy Spirit. We make far too many assumptions at times rather than knowing! For instance, the Holy Spirit can be resting on a person, while the manifestations are demonic. Simply because His presence stirs things up! Some manifestations that we credit to the Holy Spirit therefore are often not of Him at all... so we must learn not to make too many assumptions like this because we can't afford to and scripture is quite hot about this subject; "Let not then your good be evil spoken of..." *(Romans 14:16 KJV)*

Going from immaturity to maturity is permissible and acceptable. Remaining ignorant through spiritual laziness, lack of application or diligence is not. So when manifestations become questionable, especially when attributed to the Holy Spirit - we must turn to the "ancient plumb-line" from the "Ancient of Days" - the Word of God.

The Holy Spirit does not just keep resting upon the same individuals to constantly make them shudder and shake! Especially when there is no real evidence of change in their lives; we know it is the Holy Spirit because when He touches us - we never remain the same! Below is an excerpt about some "pre-millennial mania" that people were experiencing - where folks were just beginning to "experience" the things of the Spirit and how this caused some "concerned approval" by others!

TESTIMONY THEOLOGY

In his 1980 booklet, **"Charismatic Crisis,"** Anglican Renewal leader, Michael Harper noted that; "The Charismatic Renewal does not have a particularly good track record when it comes to concern for the truth. I am chiefly here reforming to the truth about Christianity. Because of its emphasis on *'testimony'* at least in its formative years, it has tended to soft-pedal, even to ignore the truth, largely out of fear that it will divide Christians rather than unite them.

Experience vs. Truth

Many Christians have in the past been caught up in sectarian battles over words and doctrines, and it has been refreshing to defuse much of that. Animosity side tracks many of the big issues which previously divided Christians, and to find a new unity in one's experience of the Holy Spirit. But such a unity is bound to last only so long as one can survive on *'testimony theology,'* and that is not for long!"[1]

Dr. Patrick Dixon also writes, "Experience is spreading and has had a major impact in Britain. In 1994, August, 1,500 people took part in the Ichthus *'Revival Camp'* at Ashburnham. Again extraordinary scenes were witnessed.

On the first night of the Grapevine Bible week in Lincoln at the end of August, around 400 out of 3,000 began laughing during the talk. On the final evening, however, the preaching was totally disrupted as a number of those on the platform began convulsing with laughter. After a number of attempts to finish on a sober and serious subject the speaker was forced finally to cut his address short and return to his seat.

These effects on Bible weeks were being monitored with interest and possibly alarm by some involved in planning the Spring Harvest weeks for April 1995, expected in planning to draw 70,000 from across all evangelical traditions - both pro- and anti-charismatic.

The question was whether Spring Harvest broad base of fellowship would survive if there were major disruptions. At a planning meeting of the worship leaders in September 1994 it was agreed that room would be made for what God was doing, while alternatives were provided on site for those wishing to worship in a more restrained atmosphere.

By the end of August 1994 all Bible weeks were now memories, but the effects on individual churches were continuing to accelerate. Ichthus made a decision to run extra receiving meetings twice every week until the end of the year. Kensington Temple was committed to doing the same throughout September, while Pioneer People in Surrey pitched a huge tent in the grounds of a local school for two weeks, for meetings almost every day at which people like John Wimber spoke."[2]

ROLLING WEEPING LAUGHING

Martin Wroe of **"The Observer"** turned up at Queen's Road Baptist Church on Wednesday evening, 31st August, to see how things were developing.

He wrote; "The congregation was rolling in the aisles, rolling and weeping and laughing and sometimes just lying there, moaning, wailing but in no pain. In other churches, they are occasionally barking, crowing like cockerels, mooing like cows, pawing the ground like bulls and more commonly, roaring like lions. But mainly they are on the church floor laughing.

Hundreds of congregations of normally staid church goers are left shaking uncontrollingably, to all appearances revelling in some killer joke that only their fellow charismatic have been let in on.

To the consternation of traditionalist and sceptics, a primitive Pentecostalism is breaking out in sophisticated Anglican churches throughout the country.

Experience vs. Truth

Tens of thousands of British churchgoers are experiencing the *'Toronto Blessing.'* At Holy Trinity Brompton, more than 2,000 people - including recent celebrity converts, such as the topless model and singer Samantha Fox - now attend services on a Sunday, including 1,200 for the evening service. The church is jammed to the rafters. Doors open at 5.45pm for the 6.30pm opening chorus, but there are queues of 500 outside by 5.30pm. Converts are split on whether Britain is on the brink of an authentic religious revival - other revivals, such as that in Wales during 1904, began with ecstasy in the pews and ended with emptying of the pubs as the Holy Spirit fell on the unholy drinkers.

Mainstream Anglicans are horrified by the enthusiasm and unsophisticated antics of adherents, while others dismiss it as P.M.T - pre-millennial tension - or mass hysteria. But the official line of the Church of England is cautious approval.

Believers in Holy Ghost power, whether laughing like hyenas or roaring like lions, dismiss the ridicule, pointing to the 'drunken' antics of the first disciples in the Book of Acts, mocked for *'taking too much wine.'*"[3]

Many people have been drawn to what is happening by intense feelings of spiritual emptiness, particularly those in leadership who have been giving out for many years. A great desire for more of God and an overwhelming hunger often comes before the experience - but when things happen, they can often surprise even those who feel they are prepared. Personally I think there has been a need of a good laugh in the Church for many years, but as a Bible Believer, *I would have cast some of those manifestations out in Jesus name!*

ENDNOTES:

1. "Charismatic Crisis: the Charismatic Renewal: Past, Present and Future" by Michael Harper, Publisher: Anglican Renewal Ministries Australia, 1980

2. "Signs of Revival" by Dr Patrick Dixon, ISBN: 0-85476-539-5, Publisher: Kingsway Pub, p58-59

3. "The Observer" by Martin Wroe, 4th September 1994

4. This "Truth for the Journey" has been taken from: https://watchersofthe4kings.com

5. Scripture references marked AMPC are taken from the Amplified® Bible (AMPC), Copyright © 1954, 1958, 1962, 1964, 1965, 1987 by The Lockman Foundation. Used by permission. www.Lockman.org

6. Scripture references marked GW are taken from GOD'S WORD®, © 1995 God's Word to the Nations. Used by permission of Baker Publishing Group.

7. Scripture references marked KJV are taken from the King James Version of the Bible.

LETTER 32

Truth for the Journey

Liberation from Segregation

Letter to the Church, 25th May 2010

*T**here is neither Jew nor Greek, slave nor free, male nor female, for you are all one in Christ Jesus. If you belong to Christ, then you are Abraham's seed, and heirs according to the promise.*

(Galatians 3:28)

We all need to love and be loved that's a fact! Inwardly we long for those rare moments of intimate heart-to-heart conversations, but often find this difficult to fulfil. For the fortunate few perhaps, we have one or two friends with whom to share in-depth thoughts. But often we are not free to love as we would like, bound by childhood hurts, irrational fears, constraints of selfishness, legalism and all the social conditioning from the world around us, helps to inhibit our freedom to love others and to be loved by them. Our ability to simply "enjoy" others is sadly but unquestionably limited.

"At the heart of the need for liberation is a longing to break free - free to love, free to be with others, to listen and cherish them. What we long for God also desires for us: to enjoy friendship, affection and community."[1]

The reality is that after generations of invariable slavery, oppression, control and prejudice, people are not loving and conversing with one another as they should. In Galatians 3:28 Paul mentions three issues of liberation in the early church involving ethnicity, social status and gender:

> *There is neither Jew nor Greek, slave nor free, male nor female, for you are all one in Christ Jesus. If you belong to Christ, then you are Abraham's seed, and heirs according to the promise.*

During that time, not unlike this, liberation needed to take place; barriers had to be removed for love to flow between people of different races, social classes and genders. Richard N. Longenecker, discusses this in the New Testament saying that Paul makes it plain,

"We are free now to converse with people of other cultures, social positions and the opposite sex. Liberation means genuine communion and ethnic, social, gender differences do not matter. That we can engage in conversation with one another without letting the differences obstruct our relationship. When open communication happens between races, social classes and sexes, we experience a foretaste of heaven. Little children, often seem free of the racial, class and gender barriers that imprison us, and we have longings for that kind of freedom ourselves to become like little children."[2]

HUMAN PLANS DISTORTED

Realistically of course, achieving this kind of liberation for ourselves is purely impossible by our own efforts. Simply because there is a wide hiatus between the longing to be free and the achieving of that freedom; the solution can only be that we need God to be at work in us *"both to will and to work his good pleasure" (see Philippians 2:13).*

All mere human plans for liberation become distorted and twisted by selfishness; history alone reminds us of how revolutions that begin with a longing for freedom quickly became sabotaged when the corruptions of power set in. We can make distinctions between healthy longings for freedom at the heart of these movements and then their outworking practices.

God is on the side of freedom and is opposed to oppression and prejudice. Therefore we regard liberation movements initially in a favourable way. We try to include them in our understanding of what God is doing in the world. But at the same time, we insist that particular longings for freedom can only be satisfied in the bigger picture of God's liberation found in the gospel.

For Paul, freedom begins in the heart and is made possible by the Spirit. Liberation begins with the freedom to engage in conversation with the three persons of the Trinity and with the neighbours we encounter. Through the Spirit there is power to overcome the bondage of the will and to be free for intimate conversation, not only with God but also across barriers of class, race and gender.

Spiritual reality is needed of all aspects of liberation, whether personal, social or political. We are all loved and forgiven because God's grace for sinners is unconditional. The opportunity to be free among other free human beings, knowing that we are loved and forgiven before we even begin - this is good news.

The beauty of this is that God is patient in His liberating of us. The apostle Paul expresses his gratitude to God in freeing him, even though he was formerly a blasphemer, a persecutor, and a man of violence.

In 1 Timothy 1:12-14 we read,

> *I thank Christ Jesus our Lord, who has given me strength, that he considered me faithful, appointing me to his service. Even though I was once a blasphemer and a persecutor and a violent man, I was shown mercy because I acted in ignorance and unbelief. The grace of our Lord was poured out on me abundantly, along with the faith and love that are in Christ Jesus.*

He says that he *(Paul)* received divine mercy because he had acted ignorantly in unbelief and that mercy overflowed into his life and changed him completely. **God's search for us is most patient and merciful. One may say no to God** a thousand times and still be forgiven and bathed in resurrection life!

ENDNOTES:

1. "A Universal Affirmation" by Jürgen Moltmann, Minneapolis, USA. Published by Fortress Press, 1992, chapter 5

2. "Social Ethics for Today" by Richard N. Longenecker, Michigan, USA. Published by Eerdmans, 1984

3. This "Truth for the Journey" has been taken from: https://watchersofthe4kings.com

4. Unless otherwise indicated, all scripture references are taken from the HOLY BIBLE, NEW INTERNATIONAL VERSION ®. NIV ®. Copyright © 1973, 1978, 1984 by the International Bible Society. Used by permission of Zondervan Publishing House. All rights reserved.

Letter 33

Truth for the Journey

Let's Make the Transition into the 21st Century

Letter to the Church, 10th August 2010

*I'm going to send you food from heaven like rain. Each day the people should go out and gather **only what they need for that day**. In this way I will test them to see whether or not they will follow my instructions.*
(Exodus 16:4 GW)

Throughout church history there have been certain pioneers who have helped mark their generation for the Lord; leaving a legacy for others to follow. Commendable - but not many of those same pioneers were able to "transition" from one move of God to the next. The transition can be crucial and just as important as the pioneering efforts to begin with.

It is not my intention here to try and cover church history in this one short letter, but I do however encourage you to go look for yourself and see what notable figures you can find of recent and not-so-recent church history, who **"moved-on" when the Spirit of God began to blow a new wind of Divine direction,** and made the transition into the "new move of God." You will find those who made the transition and those who got "lost" because somehow the past had become their logos!

CUCUMBER MENTALITY

It is wonderful to be used of God, in any generation. But we must not get stuck. So that when God wants to do a new thing, we are not stubbornly "attached" to what He did in the past. Not many have been able to "move on" throughout church history, and notoriously prefer to stay with the "familiar."

Consider the Israelites who were thinking of something as small-minded as **"onions and garlic"** when they were in the wilderness! Especially after experiencing all the adventure and enormity of God's deliverance, with the years of torment and suffering still fresh in their minds. Nonetheless they soon began to "pine" for the familiar. Listen to their murmuring and contempt,

> *If only we had meat to eat! Remember all the free fish we ate in Egypt and the cucumbers, watermelons, leeks, onions, and garlic we had? But now we've lost our appetite! Everywhere we look there's nothing but manna!*
> *(Numbers 11:4-6 GW)*

Sadly this is a common human weakness; that we begin to crave the very thing that we were set free of! We become so familiar with the "bondage" that had us captive for so long, that we actually prefer it; a re-occurrence for us all; especially if we stay in the wilderness.

It is true to say that not many people are able to "experience" God in their generation; *(pioneer, be in the "forefront")* and then move on with Him and keep the impact on the next generation alive! Instead they get stuck in the "last" move... and don't know how to "stay" with what God is doing today.

We can call this the "now move of God" *(which is relevant to any current generation...)* Most folks can only relate to their "own" experiences - so when something new happens - they can't flow with it. They miss it... lots of folks - even well intentioned folks "miss" God. *(It's easy to be "sincere" but "sincerely-wrong" at the same time!)*

PIONEERS THAT MADE IT!

By way of a short example I want to make mention of a few names that we are all so familiar with, those of recent church history; **pioneers such as Leister Sumrall, Morris Cerullo and Oral Roberts...** *(of course the list could go on...)* **Dr. Sumrall** for instance **had the likes of Howard Carter and Smith Wigglesworth as his mentors and received some of their "anointing" for his generation.** He was ordained way back in 1932 and was considered the "father" of Christian Television because he helped "secure" the "first" license for 24 hour Christian television; amongst many other achievements.

But with all of his accolades Leister was one of those men *(of his calibre)* who did not get stuck in yesteryear... he moved on... and was one of the few who was able to do so... Right up until the end, he kept "current" with his finger on the pulse of what God was doing and saying in the "now" *(remember Hebrews 11:1 calls it "now-faith!")* **There is no retirement for genuine men and woman of God!** They walk with God like Enoch did and then they are not..! They are too "black n white" to enjoy the "grey!" *(see Genesis 5:24)*

Leister kept hearing God, keeping relevant to the day that he was "in" rather than aligning himself with the "experiences" of the past *(regardless of how successful they might have been)* he kept himself aligned to God. In fact the more successful a move may have been, can prevent folks from moving on to the next wave... somehow they imagine that God could only be successful in "their" generation - no matter how long ago that was - and don't ever move on because of that premise...

To qualify this, let me say that there is always a balance to everything... we are not talking about being "politically correct" or "relevant" in that context but in regards to what "God is doing and saying today."

Dr. Sumrall was a good example for us to follow; not to get stuck in yesterday... but **stay hooked up with what God is saying and doing today.** If that means moving on from what we have known all our lives... moving away from the familiar - then yes... we must move on and not miss God. We must not get stuck in a generational or denominational rut!

If we refuse to move on with God, then what might have been "successful" in the past has now become a "deception," especially if it prevents us from hearing and moving on with God today. Reading books and studying "history" can be of great value and is great in its place. BUT... if we are so caught up in the past, that we fail to hear God for today, then we have been caught in deception. **It takes a very "brave" man or woman - to move on with God. Especially if they helped pioneer the old!**

YESTERDAY AND TODAY

Of course when we talk about "what God is saying today" this does not in any way change **His "Logos-Word"** *(written)*... this always remains the same **"yesterday, today and forever."** However His **"Rhema-Word"** - that which he **"speaks" today** - is fresh and is NOW manna. It never contradicts His written Word. But it is for today. Otherwise we would all still be wearing sackcloth and ashes!!!

Let's make sure that we move with the tide; God's tide. Not with the "popular opinion" or "political correctness" of our day; but with God. **What is He saying right now? What is on His heart for our world right now?** If we know more about previous centuries and what God said to them, than we do today, then we have "missed" God for today.

Let's not make that same mistake that so many others have made and **move on** "with" God into the 21st Century. Nothing is holding us back. **We must make the "transition"** which is only possible when we hear God's voice. "I am the good shepherd, and know my *sheep*, and am known of mine... they shall hear my voice..." *(John 10:14-16 KJV)*

ENDNOTES:

1. This "Truth for the Journey" has been taken from: https://watchersofthe4kings.com

4. Scripture references marked GW are taken from GOD'S WORD®, © 1995 God's Word to the Nations. Used by permission of Baker Publishing Group.

5. Scripture references marked KJV are taken from the King James Version of the Bible.

Letter 34

Truth for the Journey

Traditions of Man make the Word of God of no Effect!

Letter to the Church, 16th April 2010

*G**ive, and it shall be given unto you; good measure, pressed down, and shaken together, and running over, shall men give into your bosom. For with the same measure that ye mete withal it shall be measured to you again.*

(Luke 6:38)

John Avanzini says in his book, **"Always Abounding"** that it's the traditions of man that create the misunderstandings and the problems where scripture is concerned. For he says, *"See how our traditions tend to make the Word of God of no effect."*[1]

> *Making the Word of God of none effect through your tradition...*
>
> *(Mark 7:13)*

The plain teaching of the scriptures is that God is not obliged to give anything to anyone until something has been given to Him.

> *Give, and it shall be given unto you; good measure, pressed down, and shaken together, and running over, shall men give into your bosom. For with the same measure that ye mete withal* **it shall be measured to you again.**
>
> *(Luke 6:38)*

Most Christians make the mistake of considering their tithe as a *"gift"* to God. According to the bible, the tithe *belongs* to God. Those who tithe are simply returning to the Lord that which is already His. *"... **all the tithe** of the land...**is the Lord's;** it is holy unto the Lord"* (Leviticus 27:30). Not only does the tithe belong to the Lord but also it is clearly stated that it must be returned to Him in a timely manner. If not, **He charges the delinquent tither** *a very high interest rate. "And if a man will at all redeem ought (hold back any) of his tithes, he shall add thereto the **fifth** part (20%) thereof"* (Leviticus 27:31; emphasis added).

There it is in black and white. The tithe is the Lord's, and it must not be kept back from Him. If it is, **God charges twenty-percent interest!** Let this sink down into your spirit. God does not owe anyone so much *that there shall not be room enough to receive it* when they tithe. The tithe is His already. Realizing this, let me help you to see just what giving the tithe does for us. *It opens the windows of heaven.*

Traditions of Man make the Word of God of no Effect!

It is a universal practice among men to close and lock the windows and doors to keep thieves out of the house. Is it any surprise to find that God does this same thing? **As long as a person robs God of the tithe, the windows of heaven stay tightly closed over his life.** While the windows of heaven are closed, the increase of God is blocked.

Look again at God's promise to open the windows of heaven over your life each time you faithfully tithe.

> *Bring ye all the tithes into the storehouse, that there may be meat in mine house, and prove me **now** herewith, saith the Lord of hosts, **if I will not open you the windows of heaven, and pour you out a blessing...***
> (Malachi 3:10)

Every time you tithe, the windows of heaven open. God then stands ready to *pour* out a blessing. But remember... something more is needed. God says it is not enough to simply open the windows of heaven with your tithe. Everything in heaven won't just start tumbling out through those windows. The blessings must be poured out.

HOW MUCH IS THE MEETING GOING TO COST?

I like what John Avanzini says, **"God does not ask you to give your tithes and offerings to make you poor."** I remember some years ago, God was prompting me to go to one of John Avanzini's meetings and in those days my initial reaction was, *"How much is this meeting going to cost me?!"* Do you know that's true for many? They literally leave their purse or wallet at home just in case God might convict them to give! But God spoke to my heart very loudly and said, **"It's not about what you can do for me, it's about what I *(He)* can do for you."**

Listen, it's taken me years to get these revelations into my heart, into my soul and into my consciousness, THAT GOD WANTS TO BLESS US. HE WANTS TO ESTABLISH US IN HIS PROSPERITY. I can't understand how anyone would not want to receive what God has already provided for, whether it is their healing or any other need.

Your tithing *(of obedience)* opens the windows of heaven. Another word is ***"floodgates."*** I like that word, *"floodgates"* it reminds me of an enormous DAM and you are standing at the foot of this colossal wall, the other side is literally billions of gallons of water. Just imagine that, behind the floodgates of heaven, there is enough supply to furbish planet earth a million times.

It's important to remember you are giving your offerings so that God can *(and will)* pour out all of those blessings. Because now your tithe has opened the floodgate, all those blessings that you could not imagine are yours. Remember it also says that the measure that you give will also be the measure that He gives back to us. Referring more to what we see as the offering *(seed)* side of our commitment to God.

You might ask yourselves a question, which part of my giving i.e., the paying of my tithe or the giving of my offering, brings the return that God promises? **Let me just clarify again.** These steps of obedience of paying one's tithe and giving of offerings trigger **two different responses from**

Traditions of Man make the Word of God of no Effect!

God. *(We need to do all things by faith. So we need to establish that we have to believe God to bring about any response).*

> **The first response** from God is to open the heavens or the floodgates; that in *itself* does not bring the return. What it means is that heaven is open.
> **The second response** is the harvest of your seed.

Now we need just to clarify here that we are not just talking about money. And we are not looking to pay God to heal us or to bless us! But He is helping us to respond by faith to Him in every area of our lives. It also has been said that He is not looking for our money, but He is looking to get money to us! It's about **God's ways of financial release** throughout the Body of Christ to be used within this time to fuel the gospel and to enhance His work here on earth.

> **Your tithe then is a door opener. It opens a door / window(s) to the field(s) where you sow your seed that will bring you your harvest.**

ENDNOTES:

1. "Always Abounding" by John Avanzini, Published by Tyndale House Publishers, Copyright © 1983, Printed in the USA. p27
2. This "Truth for the Journey" has been taken from: https://watchersofthe4kings.com
3. Unless otherwise indicated, all scripture references are taken from the King James Version of the Bible.

LETTER 35

Truth for the Journey

Lord, Electrify the Fence!

Letter to the Church, 27th August 2010

Who here qualifies for the job of overseeing...? A person the Master can depend on to feed the workers on time each day. Someone the Master can drop in on unannounced and always find him doing his job...

(Matthew 24:45-46 MSG)

In our opening scripture Jesus was talking here about the faithful and wise "servant-ruler" or as the Amplified version *(AMPC)* says the, "faithful, thoughtful, and wise servant." We can discover through reading this scripture that "faithfulness" is a huge requirement of the Lord. Success can often come through aggression and abuse - but Christ is looking for us to succeed through "faithfulness."

This story about the "servant-ruler" applies to us all considering the fact that although we are all meant to "rule" and "reign" with Christ, we are also meant to "serve." So this scripture does not just apply to those in leadership! In fact every believer has responsibilities within the Body of Christ and within God's Kingdom; firstly towards God and then towards each another. Responsibilities that we must never "shirk" or "despise." We must be faithful.

Looking at this unfaithful servant-ruler in Matthew chapter 24 we can see that he began "calculating" that his master was not coming back and selfishly took what he could from the situation; including eventually beating his fellow servants and drinking with the drunkards. Verse 51 tells us of the "consequence" of such unfaithfulness; where Jesus Himself warns that when the master finally returns, this unfaithful servant-ruler would be cut in two! Now that's a sober reality!

If we proceed with this theme and read 1 Peter 5:1-4 we find a further description of what God is looking for in a faithful servant-ruler, "I WARN and counsel the elders among you *(the pastors and spiritual guides of the church)* as a fellow elder and as an eyewitness [called to testify] of the sufferings of Christ, as well as a sharer in the glory *(the honor and splendor)* that is to be revealed *(disclosed, unfolded)*: Tend *(nurture, guard, guide, and fold)* the flock of God that is [your responsibility], not by coercion or constraint, but willingly; not dishonorably motivated by the advantages and profits [belonging to the office], but eagerly and cheerfully; Not domineering [as arrogant, dictatorial, and overbearing persons] over those in your charge, but being examples *(patterns and models of Christian living)* to the flock *(the congregation)*. And [then] when the Chief Shepherd is revealed, you will win the conqueror's crown of glory" *(1 Peter 5:1-4 AMPC)*.

FAITHFULNESS IS THE KEY TO SUCCESS

Although lengthy the Amplified is a necessary read nonetheless as it spells out the first requirement for any such servant-ruler - "faithfulness." God is not looking for success in the way that the world comprehends it. Instead success - in God's economy of things - is faithfully carrying out the duty that He assigned for each of us to fulfil - individually and corporately.

Besides the "consequences" of unfaithfulness there are always "rewards" for faithfulness. Jesus Himself foretold this by saying, "A God-blessed man or woman, I tell you. It won't be long before the Master will put this person in charge of the whole operation!" *(Matthew 24:46-47 MSG)* In the Young's Literal Translation it says; "...verily I say to you, that *over all his substance* he will set him" *(YLT)*.

Now there is another side to this coin, as there always is; the first being "reward" and the second being "judgment." In his book, **"Prophetic Guide for the End Times,"** the late **Derek Prince** wrote; **"Faithfulness in this life leads to promotion in the next... The way we conduct ourselves in this world will determine what we will be for eternity. There is no substitute for faithfulness."**[1]

As we continue to look at Christ's return and the consequences of His coming on believers, we must not only see Him as Saviour but also as "Judge." In fact God's appointed Judge. Both Romans 14 and 2 Corinthians 5 describes the judgment seat of Christ and how He will judge the Church. During which process only two categories exist: good or evil. **Derek Prince** better articulates this by saying, **"We in the church have invented a third category: not good, but not evil either. In God's view that category does not exist. If you are not good you are evil."**[2]

This is very pointed but true! Without any shadow of doubt there are going to be consequences to the Lord's return and today there are many so called Christians who don't realize that they are sitting on a literal time bomb! Jesus' intention has always been to "return" which means the year of "Jubilee" and the year of God's favour will finally come to an end. We have as long as it takes, for Him to return, then no longer.

Even though Jesus' own disciples thought that He would return in their own day, including every successive generation after that, the signs of the times do indicate that His return is more "imminent" than ever before. Does this mean those who are still in the valley of decision about their commitment to the Lord are living on borrowed time? Yes, it could be said like that!

DON'T STRADDLE THE FENCE

In the reality of Church today, sadly **there are too many "fence-sitters!" who straddle the fence because they won't "commit" but still want to be considered "believers."** They want all the fringe-benefits that true believers enjoy, without

Lord, Electrify the Fence!

the cost of commitment. They want the trophy without the effort; the glory without the pain and wear the victors crown without any endurance or staying power! *(It takes truck-loads of perseverance, diligence and determination to truly serve the Lord, because there are too many opportunities to quit!)*

In any case those who find themselves sitting on the proverbial fence will also find themselves in a very tight spot spiritually speaking! **Derek Prince** phrases it this way, **"When the Holy Spirit comes to the Church... one of the first things that He does is to electrify the fence!"**[3] I love that! Needless to say, it is for this precise reason that so many folks *(entire churches in fact!)* don't welcome the Holy Spirit. Instead they cherish their comfort zone; their suspended position that dangles between "neutrality" and "half-heartedness!"

The evil servant-ruler who lost the vision of his master's return also lost his restraint! His behaviour altered drastically. This is true for any church. If the reality of Christ's return is not proclaimed, and the people lose sight of His coming - the ultimate standards of holiness are lost forever. God's people need to live in holiness and to walk with the Spirit of God's Holiness *(the Holy Spirit)* and for this they need a clear sight of His return. Just like the wicked servant, the alternative for us is to be led astray of our "own" lusts and degraded by our own behaviour *(see James 1:14)*. Instead we must keep His "coming" in our sights.

Consider this, according to chapter 24, when the master does finally return "unannounced," and the servant is not ready for him, he will be cut in two! The master presented here of course, is Jesus. But is He truly capable of cutting someone in two? Yes! We better believe it... for as "thorough and diligent" as Jesus is to save us, He is just as "thorough and faithful" to judge us! **If we do not commit to Him as our Saviour, we will certainly encounter Him as Judge.**

I leave you with this final thought. In Matthew 13:42 it talks about "tares" of wheat in the field - this is referring to people. Tares look exactly like wheat - but are sterile *(barren)* never "producing" anything! People can be like this. They go to church their whole lives; looking like all the other believers but never truly "entering-in" for themselves. They live so close, right in the midst of it all, but never partake and never truly commit. For them, scripture tells us that there will be "weeping and gnashing of teeth," simply because they were "so-near-and-yet-so-far."

To close - how should we remedy this? Set up "fence-sitters-anonymous" or as Pastors and Leaders allow the Holy Spirit to *"electrify the fence?!"* It's certainly going to get exciting, one way or another! **No one can be neutral, not ever.** There are only two categories that exist: good or evil *(life or death)* and "everyone" must choose! *(See Deuteronomy 30:19)*

ENDNOTES:

1. "Prophetic Guide to the End Times: Facing the Future without Fear" by Derek Prince, Copyright © 2008, Published by Chosen Books. Printed in the USA. p100
2. Ibid
3. Ibid (p100-101)
4. This "Truth for the Journey" has been taken from: https://watchersofthe4kings.com
5. Scripture references marked AMPC are taken from the Amplified® Bible (AMPC), Copyright © 1954, 1958, 1962, 1964, 1965, 1987 by The Lockman Foundation. Used by permission. www.Lockman.org
5. Scripture quotations marked MSG are taken from The Message. Copyright © 1993, 1994, 1995, 1996, 2000, 2001, 2002. Used by permission of NavPress Publishing Group.
6. Scripture quotations marked YLT are taken from the Young's Literal Translation of the bible.

❖

Letter 36

Truth for the Journey

Don't Lose Sight of Honour

Letter to the Church, 9th April 2010

*R*ender to all men their dues... respect to whom respect is due, and honour to whom honour is due.
(Romans 13:7 AMPC)

The concept of honour in modern western and secular society has declined a lot in recent times. But concepts of honour do still exist and vary widely between cultures; in fact each culture or society has their own code of honour, including those notorious "honour-killings" of certain cultures of whose families have felt that their honour has been "defiled" in some way.

Less severely of course, for most cultures and countries the term **honour** can simply refer to dignity, office and reputation, even fame or position that has been earned rewarded with certain honours of State, such as ceremony, title or decoration; particularly military or political honours. Still, more typically are civilian awards or honours such as the British OBE or knighthood or alternatively membership of the French Légion d'honneur!

Then of course honour can mean specific things for different genders or people groups, for example, both typically and historically honour for a woman has meant chastity, sexual purity/virginity *(and in the case of married women, "fidelity")*.

Historically in ancient Japan, honour was always seen as a duty by the *Samurai*. When one lost their honour, the only possible way to retrieve it was by death! So honour can be a relative term with a wide variety of concepts behind it, depending on collective cultures, ethics and beliefs.

DEFINING HONOUR

However better related to this segment, is the honour that relates to character and behaviour as a believer in Christ! *Latin* for honour is simply *"honor, or honoris."* Different meanings include: trustworthiness, character, honesty, respect, worth and stature; fairness and integrity of action; sincerity, possessing high moral principles and the absence of deceit or fraud.

Honour in a regular dictionary also includes: worship *(to the Supreme Being)*, nobility of soul, magnanimity, virtuous conduct and personal integrity, honour in relationship, reputation, respect and moral or ethical excellence.

However when we look into the scriptures, honour is given very specific terms in both Greek and Hebrew such as: "heavy or weighty; splendour and glory." It means "to value or to highly esteem *(of the highest degree)*, to revere, to prize; precious and dignity itself;" integrity, credibility and even elegance. But to be "without honour" is to be "despised."

So it's easy to see that from a variety of sources, in both secular and scriptural sources, honour can have a manifold set of meanings. But I prefer the basic scriptural meanings. Especially that which denotes weight! You know when someone is called to preach and when they are not! They bring a weight into the room with them. Their words carry weight and the atmosphere is usually heavy with the anointing! Whereas, when there is *no weight* behind what someone says it usually denotes that they are not anointed for that job or don't have the authority for it. Rather they have assumed it! This is the difference between being "called or appointed!" *(Remember that many are called but **few** are chosen!)*

I see people today who are preaching when they should be singing and vice versa. Folk have prophesied over them and they have launched out into preaching ministries when they should stick to what they do best. The "weight" is behind their singing rather than their preaching because that's what they are anointed for!

Let me add, there is room for *singers-turned-preachers* of course. But it must be God ordained and not humanly manufactured. "Preaching" is simply not the same as "entertainment" and it does not have the same *crowd-pleasing effect!* In fact the two are worlds apart; especially when someone tries to run with an apostolic "office" when no one has qualified them for such. They call themselves apostles because they travel and share insights... When only last year they were singing! *(It's comical or should I say commercial?)* Anyway, there is no weight behind it...

Even my dentist has "weight." He is *authorised (been given authority)* to touch my teeth. No one else, thank you! Especially no one fresh out of college, without his years of experience! I suppose a good scripture that would best fit here would be Romans 13:7 *(AMPC);*

> *Render to all men their dues... respect to whom respect is due, and honour to whom honour is due.*

Honour here means: to esteem "especially in the highest degree" *(Strong's #G5099)*[1] and dignity. Scripture also tells us to "Honour thy father and thy mother, as the Lord thy God hath commanded thee; that thy days may be prolonged, and that it may go well with thee..." *(Deuteronomy 5:16; Exodus 20:12)*

HONOUR PROLONGS LIFE

The collective meanings of the Hebrew word used here for honour include: "promote, glorify and to make a weighty and heavy boast!" And the same meaning is used in 1 Samuel 2:30, "...for them that honour me I will honour, and they that despise me shall be lightly esteemed." Again the same Hebrew word for honour is used also in Proverbs 3:9 "Honour the Lord with thy substance, and with the firstfruits of all thine increase" which also denotes, "to be rich!"

But in Ephesians 6:1-3 it says, *"...**obey your parents in the Lord:** for this is right. **Honour** thy father and mother; (which is the first commandment with promise;) That it may be well with thee, and thou mayest live long on the earth."* And this means, "to *prize*, to value and to *revere.*" And your parents ***"in the Lord"*** are those very people who are in authority over you and must give an account for you. God provided such for you; you don't have an orphan spirit remember!

Only those who want to be orphaned are those who don't want to accept the role of or to honour their spiritual parents. However to balance everything, let me say this... we must know how to give honour and how to receive it, even who to give it to and who to receive it from. A good indication is given in the very words of Christ in John 5:41-44.

I receive not honour from men... How can ye believe, which receive honour one of another, and seek not the honour that cometh from God only.

If we give honour to whom honour is due, *(those legitimately placed over us by the Lord)*, and look to receive honour from God not from others... then we won't go far wrong!

But in a world where we want to explain everything in terms of psychology and throw scripture out the window when it pleases us... we find that even preachers will rant over those selective scriptures that seem to benefit them the most... simple proof of that, is the fact that you hardly ever hear endless ranting over "honouring spiritual parents in the Lord!"

That's because everyone wants to *free-style-it* in the Kingdom; to go it alone. Everyone wants to receive honour from men but not many want to give it. But if we are wise enough to discern many other things... then let us not lose use of our discerner when it comes to who to "honour" and who not to. Consider this... if you have no one to honour as spiritual parents... then it stands to reason that you must have orphaned yourself and become a spiritual bastard.

Don't forget to honour today and to give honour where it is due and not just where it will benefit you in the temporal. And when you honour your parents IN THE LORD remember that you are doing it **unto the Lord** more than you do it unto men. Keep it in perspective and don't lose sight of honour.

> *BUT UNDERSTAND this, that in the last days will come (set in) perilous times of great stress and trouble [hard to deal with and hard to bear].*
>
> *For people will be lovers of self and [utterly] self-centered, lovers of money and aroused by an inordinate [greedy] desire for wealth, proud and arrogant and contemptuous boasters. They will be abusive (blasphemous, scoffing), disobedient to parents, ungrateful, unholy and profane.*
>
> *[They will be] without natural [human] affection (callous and inhuman), relentless (admitting of no truce or appeasement); [they will be] slanderers (false accusers, troublemakers), intemperate and loose in morals and conduct, uncontrolled and fierce, haters of good.*
>
> *[They will be] treacherous [betrayers], rash, [and] inflated with self-conceit. [They will be] lovers of sensual pleasures*

and vain amusements more than and rather than lovers of God.

For [although] they hold a form of piety (true religion), they deny and reject and are strangers to the power of it [their conduct belies the genuineness of their profession].
(2 Timothy 3:1-5 AMPC)

FORWARD OR PASS IT ON!

Note: If this book has blessed you, let it bless others. Share it, and let the message bear fruit in someone else's life. *"What you have heard... entrust to... others" (2 Timothy 2:2).* Why not sow by gifting a copy, or even placing a bundle in the hands of your home group or church? In this way the truth multiplies and glorifies our Heavenly Father.

A massive Thank You

ENDNOTES:

1. Strong, James. S.T.D., L.L.D. 1890. Strong's Exhaustive Concordance, Dictionaries (Lexicon) of the Hebrew and Greek Words

2. This "Truth for the Journey" has been taken from: https://watchersofthe4kings.com

3. Unless otherwise indicated, all scripture references are taken from the King James Version of the Bible.

4. Scripture references marked AMPC are taken from the Amplified® Bible (AMPC), Copyright © 1954, 1958, 1962, 1964, 1965, 1987 by The Lockman Foundation. Used by permission. www.Lockman.org

Leaders Feedback Testimonies

Disclaimer: For the most part these testimonies *(writen feedback)* have been unedited by us and therefore remain in the original vernacular of each individual, *(in their own style of speech/native dialect)*. We prefer authenticity to perfection! Please bear this in mind when reading. Thank you.

"Thanks very much for this encouraging revelation. I promise to keep in touch every time I find access to mail."
Ayuk, Cameroon

"God bless you Dr Pateman, for such a message of transformation. I am blessed always with your teaching."
Leonard, Germany
(in response to "Happiness begins between your Ears," 26th February 2010)

"Praise the Lord so much for all the emails you have been sending to me, there are a great encouragement."
Pastor Robert and Topista Nangoli, Uganda
(in response to "Worry is Practical Atheism," 2nd March 2010)

"Thanks Brother for your teaching, they bless my soul and not only me even those I share with. Thanks and bless you."
Aloysious Luswata, Uganda
(in response to "Worry is Practical Atheism," 2nd March 2010)

TRUTH FOR THE JOURNEY

"Just wish God's immense blessings on you and the ministry. Had a wonderful time meditating on the newsletter. It was indeed a 'Truth for the journey.' Thanks very much for the rhema."
Youbi Sandrine, Cameroon
(in response to "Worry is Practical Atheism," 2nd March 2010)

"Allow me to thank you for all the inspiring messages you send unto me, in fact they have been good and helpful to my Christian life. Thanks to you and I appreciate a lot."
Ssesanga Gerald Paul, Uganda

"Hello Dr Pateman; I have been blessed a lot by a series of your letters, articles and publications, which you sent to me. I really want to express my gratitude to God for these e-mails."
Pastor Akowe
(in response to "Worry is Practical Atheism," 2nd March 2010)

"Bishop, understand that we do pray for you, many messages from you have blessed us, I can't forget the true Christmas message you sent, it changed and blessed us! So we trust many and many are blessed. We hesitate to reply to your messages knowing that you have many that email you and you have a lot to do so, we take in what you teach, bless the Lord God and pray for to continually be used by Him for His own glory.

We thank God for who He is and for what we're in Him through Jesus Christ our Lord and Savior. Much love from Adonai Family."
Aloysious and Abishage, Uganda
(in response to "Worry is Practical Atheism," 2nd March 2010)

"I enjoyed your writing."
Apostle Donald Thompson, Louisiana, United States
(in response to "Have You been Called or Appointed?" 6th March 2010)

"Dear Bishop Dr., I want to thank God for you and the message you have. I am blessed because of you. We are together in prayer, we promise you that as Pool of Life Conquerors Church we will continue to pray for you, for God to continue to use you in power. Thank you my pastor and bishop, may the good God bless you, and yours.

Thank you also my dear Bishop to take care for my life and ministry; you always write for me, God bless you."
Your Son, Bishop Ssentongo Elly Blest, Uganda

"Dearest in Christ, thanks for your wonderful words of encouragement, may the good Lord bless you and your family and may your ministry expound more and more in Jesus Name, Amen."
Teddy
(in response to "Destiny in Our Mouths," 9th March 2010)

"Dear Pastor Alan, thanks for these wonderful newsletter that you have sent. They are very helpful to me and ministry. I will learn a lot from you, I thank God for connecting me to you."
Pastor Duncan Nyozani, Malawi
(in response to "Our God Given Antidote To Stress!" 23rd March 2010)

"Amen! Great Lesson! They are such a Blessing & Inspiration. Thank You!"
Lana Finley
(in response to "Destiny in Our Mouths," 9th March 2010)

"Beloved, Just wish to send you words of thanks for the weekly letters forwarded to me. I am praying for you and hope to visit you some day."
Cyril J. Iroh, Cameroon

"Shalom, you're a great source of blessing to us here in Nigeria. Thanks for being a blessing to us."
Pastor Tom Etinosa, Nigeria
(in response to "The Cancer of Chaos and Spiritual Anarchy," 26th March 2010)

"Hello Sir, I am so pleased to read the article related to cancer, I am so impressed to read it, I love God and He loves me lot. I am really so pleased. God Bless you."
Victor Jacob, Pakistan
(in response to "The Cancer of Chaos and Spiritual Anarchy," 26th March 2010)

"Dear Dr. of our Lord Jesus, You have been an inspiration. Thanks."
Evangelist Charles Mboh, Cameroon
(in response to "The Cancer of Chaos and Spiritual Anarchy," 26th March 2010)

"Dear Respected brother Alan, Greetings from Nepal. Thank you again for your unconditional love, constant prayer and encouragement. We pray that God would continue to bless you, your family and ministries. We all are well, all the works that we are involved in are going well, Praise be to His Holy Name."
Pastor Krishna Pariyar, Nepal

"Thank you I am grateful. Remain blessed in Jesus name (amen). Best wishes."
Abdul Izegue
(in response to "Victory over Death," 2ⁿᵈ April 2010)

"Thanks indeed for your great mail on 'The Truth for the Journey.' What a blessing this is. Our victory in CHRIST is utter truth. GOD bless you."
Brother Kolle George Nkume, Cameroon
(in response to "Victory over Death," 2ⁿᵈ April 2010)

"I just love your essays. They happen to come exactly when needed. Used them as a testimony for what I preached to others, like my Muslim employees. Great Blessings."
Silke Gerdes, Germany
(in response to "Never Be Denied," 6ᵗʰ April 2010)

"Glory to God in the name of our heavenly father, I used to read your message and share with my family & church. The matter I'm getting specially I'm sharing with my orphanage children. They are very good in nature and very soft in their behaviour. Please pray for them."
John Shaw, Nepal
(in response to "Never Be Denied," 6ᵗʰ April 2010)

"Greetings in the precious name of our Lord and Saviour Jesus Christ. I was blessed and encouraged by the Newsletter you sent me on 'Truth for the Journey.' May the Almighty God add you more wisdom to continue strengthening the church through these edifying scriptures. Thank you."
Robert Opila, Ministry Director Bible League Uganda
(in response to "Never Be Denied," 6ᵗʰ April 2010)

"Thanks for today's message. It's so encouraging. Please keep up the good work. Greetings to you from the church and ministry friends in Uganda. We love you and pray for you always. Sharing the mission."
Isaac Mugabi, Uganda
(in response to "Honour," 9ᵗʰ April 2010)

"Thanks Alan for your word. May His hand continue to lead you to further glorify His name."
Jordan Kwong, Malaysia
(in response to "Traditions of Men," 16ᵗʰ April 2010)

Leaders Feedback Testimonies

"Dr. Alan Pateman, Blessings! Thank you for your message. I like it, God bless you and your ministry. Yours in His Services."
Pastor Nawaz Bhatti, Pakistan
(in response to "Kingdom Reign of God," 20th April 2010)

"Thanks for your messages. They are such a blessing. More grace in Jesus name."
Pastor Folarin Alonge, Ph.D., Nigeria
(in response to "True Prosperity is about Giving," 27th April 2010)

"Dr. Alan, thanks so much for this piece & the conclusive prayer point. God bless you in Jesus Mighty Name, amen. I have always believed in the place of 'tithe of tithes' and I practice it with the Church as the Senior Pastor & go further in 'first fruits.'"
Pastor Femi Olupitan, Nigeria
(in response to "Responsible to Tithe the Tithe!" 30th April 2010)

"Dear Dr Alan Pateman, Receive greetings from us here in Enkhuizen, Holland. Thank you for your encouraging messages. Your brother in Christ and in His service for the lost."
Peter Gatete, Netherlands
(in response to "Break Out," 4th May 2010)

"Good day Dr. Alan Pateman for today's message, may the good Lord increase you and the ministry more and more. Amen in Jesus Name."
Pastor Tony Orhue
(in response to "ALMS: A Vital Decision," 11th May 2010)

"I am grateful to God who made it possible for me to enjoy this write up of yours today. It's great to know that in giving alms (not minding the size thereof) a man gets to be more like God the father of light who gave us so much and yet crowned his giving with the gift of his only son-JESUS CHRIST. God bless you indeed in Jesus name. (Amen)"
Oyebanji Roseline
(in response to "ALMS: A Vital Decision," 11th May 2010)

"Hi Apostle, What a marvellous teaching! I couldn't stop myself laughing out loudly over the last two sentences: 'Don't be deluded, no one can get drunk on your ten pence! Don't let nonsense thinking hinder your compassion or stop your giving.' Thank you for this exposee. Could you also bring some enlightenment on the subject of Seed-sowing at sometime please? Sincere regards."

Andrew Donkor-Bosie, UK England
(in response to "ALMS: A Vital Decision," 11th May 2010)

"Dr. Alan Pateman, Blessings, Thank you for your writings and messages very inspirational and excited for me and my church too. All these views are laying maximum impact. God bless you and use more and more."
Pastor Nawaz Bhatti, Pakistan
(in response to "Victims or Investors," 18th May 2010)

"Dear Alan, Greetings in the name of our savior Lord Jesus Christ. I am very thankful to for these messages. I am blessed with them. God bless you."
Ather Javed, Pakistan
(in response to "Appropriating God's Word," 4th June 2010)

"I'm glad to have you both as friends as brothers and sisters in the body of Christ. The message of Queen Sheba was on point, be blessed, our family loves you in Christ."
Sandy Combs
(in response to "Appropriating God's Word," 4th June 2010)

"Dear Dr. Alan, Your teaching where I learned of the word of God, I already shared unto these tribal village people. We will also pray for you, mainly the children. God Bless You More. You are in our hearts Dr. Alan. Blessings."
Rodrigo Limpot, Philippines
(in response to "The Winners Life – Part 1," 15th June 2010)

"Dear Dr. Alan Pateman, we are very grateful to write you this email. We thank God for your teachings we are receiving. Your messages are helping us, changing our lives. This is causing the work of God to grow fast and we are not the same. My request to you is that, you may have a bible school here in Malawi so that you can help more leaders to sustain in God's work. Please, we are blessed with your teachings, continue sending us. May God bless you. Yours in Christ Jesus."
Apostle Peter & Naomi Simbi, Malawi
(in response to "The Winners Life – Part 1," 15th June 2010)

"Dear Alan, I would like to thank you for your write up, 'Truth for the Journey.' It came at a perfect moment for our ministry. The Lord continue to richly bless you and your ministry."
Rev. J. Daley, UK England
(in response to "Leadership Seductions Series – Staying Accountable," 25th June 2010)

Leaders Feedback Testimonies

"A good one, thanks so much! You are a blessing."
Lawrence Egharevba, Nigeria
(in response to "Leadership Seductions Series – Deliverance from Parasites," 29th June 2010)

"Dear Dr Pateman, I wish to express my appreciation for these life changing teachings. Just like they are tagged 'Truth for the journey.' I believe we need much of these today in the Body of Christ! God bless you real good for all you're doing for His glory. Every blessing."
Pastor Peter Asiazobor, Italy
(in response to "Leadership Seductions Series – Deliverance from Parasites," 29th June 2010)

"Respected Sir, praise the Lord, I want to thank you very-very much for your email teachings to my id. I am so blessed for your preaching and teachings to my email. Sir this is Pastor Amar Batia from Shimla. I want you to pray for us and pray for our needs. May God bless you richly."
Pastor Amar Batia, India
(in response to "Leadership Seductions Series – Humanism vs. the Spirit of God," 2nd July 2010)

"Greetings my dear respectful brother, My dear brother, I learn many things by your and by your these all qualities and abilities I improve myself. Today my prayer is that my God of host bless you with more wealth, owner in your country, and received in your all life love by every one in Jesus name. I put the blood of Jesus on you, your house, boundaries, resources, income, friendship, business, life partner and whatever you have. I hope our friendship, ministerial relationship will be for the glory of God and for us and the others all Christians. Take care yourself for Jesus kingdom. Please keep me in your prayers and forever under your love. Thanks."
Your brother, Bishop Altaf Anthony, Pakistan
(in response to "Leadership Seductions Series – Humanism vs. the Spirit of God," 2nd July 2010)

"Dear Dr. Pateman, thanks for the very wonderful and educative Message 'TRUTH FOR THE JOURNEY.' May God bless you with more insight/wisdom, to continue being a blessing to others. Indeed I'm being blessed and renewed every time I go through the messages. In Christ service."
Pastor Pinka L. Gold
(in response to "Destiny in our Mouths," 9th March 2010)

"Pastor. Praise God so much, thank you for your daily updates to my mail though I may not reply, I read them and they minister a lot to my spirit. Am very blessed by your mails. May God richly bless your ministry."
Sylvie Emalu

"Thank you. God bless."
Pastor Folarin Alonge, Ph.D., Nigeria
(in response to "The Strength of His Love," 13th July 2010)

"Excellent!!! Thanks for sharing this powerful message!"
Billie B. Boatwright, Oklahoma, United States
(in response to "The Python Spirit is sent to Strangle our Success!" 18th July 2010)

"Good morning Dr Alan, I am a junior pastor and your teachings have helped a lot in my ministry."
Fred
(in response to "The Python Spirit is sent to Strangle our Success!" 18th July 2010)

"This is impossible to download...that is how significant this article is. Recently reading Kim Clement on the same subject so timely for us now having entered into the realm of business the warfare is of an intense and ceaseless nature, seeking to overwhelm and suffocate us, making us weary...your word comes as a prophetic laser where it shines it liberates, the enemy doesn't want me to download this..."
David Angus, UK England
(in response to "The Python Spirit is sent to Strangle our Success!" 18th July 2010)

"This is so good... need to read it over and over..."
Maria Spiess, Ohio, United States
(in response to "Main Stream Christians vs. Disciples," 20th July 2010)

"Hello Dr Alan, thanks very much for the article, I really appreciate and I do use these article with our church congregation and we are really blessed to have you over there. May God richly bless you. Yours in Christ."
Ap. Gerald Lutalo (*Faith Ministries International*), Kampala, Uganda
(in response to "Don't Speak until God gives you the Key," 10th August 2010)

"Another powerful word, practical and like a strong grip of challenge and encouragement, to be applied and reapplied again and again after the reminder."
David Angus, UK England
(in response to "The Perils of Fear," 13th August 2010)

Leaders FeedbackTestimonies

"Greetings in the Mighty Name of our Lord and Savior Jesus Christ. I am personally blessed and encouraged whenever I read 'Truth for the Journey' that you normally send to me especially on 'The Perils of Disappointment.' This is a practical lesson to all people who are called by God to be an encouragement to themselves and to others in times of test with disappointment.

May the Lord add you more wisdom as you meditate upon Him for more inspiring messages for the strengthening of the body of Christ. Thank you."
Pastor Opila Robert *(Ministry Director Bible League Uganda)*
(in response to "The Perils of Disappointment," 20th August 2010)

"I have been receiving your mails online, 'Truth of the Journey' which have been a blessing to us in many ways. Please, continue mailing because this is what has attracted me to this ministry. Also, this is why I want to be part of this meeting in November. Yours faithfully."
Pastor James H. Mwasame, Kenya

"Hello and praise the Lord, thanks so much for the powerful messages you send to me, may the Lord continue to lift you and the ministry, you may not know how you are affecting the lives of many through these messages. It is my prayer that you plan to meet our city elders, pastors, and Church leaders for a conference. I know the staff you have it will be a blessing and they will appreciate so much, our connection is for the glory of the Lord. Thanks and God bless. Yours in Christ's vineyard."
Apostle Allan Mugoha, Eldoret, Kenya

"Dear Dr. Alan Pateman, Warm Greetings from the Andaman Islands. It was such an encouragement to read the work of the Holy Spirit through the generations. I really have been touched and there is a stronger confidence in my heart that God who continues His work will Transfer that Anointing to the next Generation. The Mantle is to be given to the next Elisha.

Please pray that there would be an Awakening in the Andaman Islands, where we have been serving God for 22 years, but still did not see a breakthrough. In Christ."
Pastor Varughese Mathew, Andaman Islands
(in response to "Passing the Baton between Generations," 3rd September 2010)

TRUTH FOR THE JOURNEY

"Thanks man of God for the messages you have been sending to me. They have been of great inspiration to me and my family. I thank God who has connected us together and I know that He has great plans ahead of time. May the God of Abraham, Isaac and Jacob bless you Richly."
Alfred Kyalo
(in response to "Our Supernatural 'Grace-Thing!'" 10th September 2010)

"Thank you, I really need more of these and Jesus in my life."
Chancy Msiska
(in response to "Self-Exaltation Denies Grace," 14th September 2010)

"So powerful a fellowship. To be honest with you, Dr, I hardly read these days. But this has so inspired me that I am forwarding it to everyone, possibly. Great writings. May the Great God Himself continue to reveal himself to you. I'm looking forward to another time of fellowship either here in the UK or over there in Germany. Stay blessed."
Pastor Albert Ransford Asiedu, UK England
(in response to "The Fellowship of the Holy Spirit," 1st October 2010)

"Thank you so much, it was such a blessing to read this subject. It has encouraged me to re-start my journaling in desiring a closer walk with the Holy Spirit."
Cheryll Skinner
(in response to "Truth: Cultivating a Deep Daily Fellowship with the Holy Spirit," 5th October 2010)

"Dr Alan, I am so blessed with your insightful, inspiring, instructive messages. I consider it as a revelational key for living a profitable life in God's kingdom. What can one do without the Holy Spirit. The operational manager of God's kingdom. The one that has the key of revelation to access the deep things of God. Thank you and I look forward to a fruitful relationship between your ministry and ours someday."
Bishop Duncan Philip
President and Founder of "Word of Love Freedom Outreach Ministries Worldwide" a.k.a "Freedom Chapel"
(in response to "Experience vs. Truth," 15th October 2010)

"Dear Dr, Thank you for your many articles. It has been a help to the church in Liberia. We are praying for you every day to plan a visit to us to help our churches."
Bishop Seleweyan
(in response to "The Strength of His Love," 20th October 2010)

Leaders FeedbackTestimonies

"Dear Servant of God, Thanks very much for the teachings that you have been sending to us, for they have been a blessing to our small growing ministry."
Pastor Rabson Sagana, Kenya
(in response to "The Kingdom Reign of God," 22nd October 2010)

"Refreshing as always."
Colin Pearson, UK England
(in response to "Is the Ecumenical Movement Promoting 'NEW DAYS - NEW WAYS?" 26th October 2010)

"I utterly enjoy your newsletters. May God continue to inspire you to share his good news and his truth."
Bishop Ralph Dennis
(in response to "'Preparation' - for Marriage not Promiscuity!" 5th November 2010)

"Dear Dr. Alan, Thanks for the wonderful work you are doing around the world. Indeed you are my mentor and not only to me but you are the mentor to my entire family. In this case I request that you consider us with one of the books you have written for us to translate in our local language in order to help our local church leaders to read by themselves. For your information we are using your teachings in our Discipleship training centers in Uganda, Southern Sudan and Democratic Republic of Congo."
Pastor Loyep Pinka Gold, Uganda
(in response to "The Paradox of Sex Education Unveiled," 9th November 2010)

"Very relevant, crucial subject. We must face up to the severe temptations of new age pornographers in a honest open way."
Colin Pearson, UK England
(in response to "Sex Will Be Prominent In The End Times," 16th November 2010)

"Thanks for the newsletter. God bless you"
Pastor Duncan Nyozani, Malawi
(in response to "Such Numbness Exists Today, that nothing 'Shocks' Anymore and Sin no longer 'Offends!'" 26th November 2010)

"Wow... How nice the message is... Thanks 4 your kindness Sir... God bless u."
Rhose
(in response to "The Abnormal Sexual Behaviour of the End Times?" 1st December 2010)

"Hi Dr. Alan, Thanks for the wonderful and powerful message. Indeed you are my mentor. Many blessings."
Pastor Pinka, Southern Sudan
(in response to "Perverted Sexuality - as Seen in the Bible!" 3rd December 2010)

"God is Great! You are such a blessing! I thank you for all that you are doing. Thanks again."
Samuel Opingo, Kenya
(in response to "Standing by Truth vs. Finger Point," 10th December 2010)

"Hello Dr. Alan Pateman, May God bless you and your congregation. Thanks for your email. Happy new year. I am very much motivated from your holy message and hope that we will continue our contact in the future. I am a senior pastor and founder and chairman of 'Spiritual United Gospel Ministries of Pakistan.' We will remember you in our prayer. May God bless you all. Your brother in Christ."
Senior Pastor Saleem Azhar, Pakistan
(in response to "The Origin of Christmas vs. Blended Traditions," 23rd December 2010)

"Simple and well put!!! Thank you!"
Billie B. Boatwright, Oklahoma, United States
Holy Ground International, Inc.
(in response to "Introduction to Leadership," 7th January 2011)

"Dear Dr Alan Pateman, Greetings in the Lord, happy new year. Am so much thankful for the news letter I have received from you, am so much inspired just after going through. Indeed this is the truth that the Holy Ghost has revealed through you, yes the Church of Christ is a not a denomination nor a material building, but it's formed up by the body of Christ. All of us belong to this body, Jesus will not take any religion during his second coming but will take up his Church.

To end up, I would you to continue sending more lessons on leadership, we have a high need to train up our local pastors and Christian lay workers here. Am based in Kenya East Africa and located in the western part of the Country. May this 2011 be full of blessings in your ministry. Hope to hear from you soon. Yours Sincerely in His service."
Pastor Eliud, Kenya
(in response to "Introduction to Leadership," 7th January 2011)

"Thank you so much for such powerful truths being released in this generation to heal save and equip the church. I am a founder and a pastor with Word of Life Mission in Kenya, East Africa and am so blessed with this very rare teachings revelations revealed. I kindly want more, how can I get to you or get more of this Teaching?

One of main God given assignments is to equip the church leaders in the Rural parts of Africa and such teachings will be so beneficial to the Body of Christ here, please keep in touch I promise to be on my knees for this ministry. May the Lord greatly bless you and your ministry. In Christ's service."
Pastor Enock Ambokah, Word of Life Mission, Kenya
(in response to "The Kingdom Reign of God," 22nd January 2011)

"Thanks Pateman for the good work of Educator and a teacher of the word of God. God bless you and keep you."
Pastor Samwel Chuchu, Kenya

"You are a blessing to this generation, I am grateful to God to know someone like you. Yes you must manifest in 2011.Thank you forever, you will remain so close, may the Lord divinely establish you this year it's a dawn of a new day in a new season. How beautiful are the feet of those that bless others. In 2011 you will manifest and shine like the sun to those who wrote you off."
Pastor Massoda Moise, Cameroon

"Dear Dr Alan, Greetings. It was good reading the message on the Kingdom of God and I have been very much blessed by the same. God bless you and keep it up before Him.
Apostle Peter Akeck
(in responds to "Kingdom Identified," 25th January 2011)

"Dear Dr. Alan, Thank you for your teaching of the word that made us strong in times like these. Another typhoon is now heading to our place. Be with us please that God sustains our needs in times like this in SUPERNATURAL WAYS. Blessings."
Rev. Rodrigo Limpot, Philippines

"Hello Rev Pateman greetings to you from Uganda, indeed I enjoy reading your writings, thank you for all the communication. May God increase you and your ministry."
Pastor Robert Muyiinza, Uganda
(in response to "Discernment of Gifting," 8th February 2011)

"My Husband/Pastor has been teaching on 'The Spirit of Discernment' now for approx. 6 weeks, hitting every part. The teaching has been awesome, and to see it on your page as well is even more awesome. IT LETS ME KNOW THAT GOD IS SPEAKING TO THE BODY OF CHRIST AS A WHOLE. Not just Kingdom Living Ministries in Detroit, but beyond. God Bless."
Constance Hamilton, Michigan, United States
(in response to "Discernment of Gifting," 8th February 2011)

"Thanks a lot Doctor for the great work you are doing for the Lord. Pray for my Ministry in Lira Northern Uganda."
Pastor David Okello, Uganda
(in response to "Establishing Leadership," 1st February 2011)

"Hi man of God, how are you doing, I am Pastor Simon Muvengei pastor and founder of Glory Evangelism church in Africa, running three churches now, but not big churches. You have been blessings to me through (Truth for the Journey) and I want you too to be blessings here in East Africa Kenya. Can you make plan to come here this year?"
Pastor Simon Muvengei, Kenya

"This is an awesome read!!! Keep on Dr. Alan & Jenny, only true leaders will vision such series."
Apostle Eugene Nchaw, Germany
(in response to "Humanism vs. the Spirit of God, Leadership Seduction Series," 3rd July 2010)

"Very very powerful message... need it for India..."
Pastor Spurgeon, India
(in response to "Deliverance from Parasites!" 22nd February 2011)

"Greetings Dr. Alan, I am Samba Gilbert in Cameroon. Just want to appreciate you and your prophetic ministry for the wonderful messages you have always emailed to me. They have indeed been nourishing especially this last one talking about DOUBT. It was not only nourishing but TIMELY.

I was presently caught in "THINKING TWO DIFFERENT THINGS AT THE SAME TIME." You just let me know I should not expect to receive anything from God unless I put that DOUBT AWAY and FIX my mind on one thing (the right one). Thank you Man of God and God richly bless your ministry. Please Keep the Letters Coming."

Leaders FeedbackTestimonies

Samba Gilbert, Cameroon
(in response to "The Perils of Double Mindedness, Doubt & Unbelief," 18th March 2011)

"Beloved Dr. Alan. My name is Emilio Sevilla from Spain and I am doing the Apostolic Work planting new churches and also helping them to be established. I have enjoyed your article and I do also teach on the apostolic with similar conclusions. If you allow me, the word Apostle means 'send to establish' because the word is made of two words which are APO-STELLO, APO to be send forth STELLO to establish. That is why Apostles should not rest until they have established the Kingdom in an area, and as you say, if there are more than one, they must work together. Thanks, God bless you."
Pr. Emilio Sevilla Lorenzo, Spain
(in response to "Marks of an Apostle," 8th April 2011)

"Dr. Alan & Jenny on a Mission, Great job man of God amen. Series on the Apostolic seemed dynamic."
Apostle Eugene Nchaw, Germany
(in response to "Truth: The Blood Transfer," 18th March 2010)

"I was inspired by your two messages. Since I have been wrestling with this commitment over a period of time and I too have asked myself that same question. God has given me by His Grace the power to disarm the enemy but as I pray I feel a great resistance and a heaviness even to exhaustion like sluggishness. I have come to realize the trench warfare-like struggle and I see that it is done inch by inch some time. There are phases to reaching the objective.

I take this opportunity to thank you for your teachings since they are very inspiring and I feel the strength in them I have always had a particular heart-felt thing for revival in this land. 'Thy Kingdom come Thy will be done.' I desire to reach that target through the will of God the Father by His Holy Spirit and by my friend the only True Intercessor Jesus Christ of Nazareth! May you be guided in your teachings by the Holy Spirit with His revelation blessings fall upon you and your family and ministry in this land."
Margaret Ghiandoni, Italy
(in response to the T4J teaching articles on Intercession, May/June 2011)

"Dear Dr. Pateman, Greetings in Jesus name! Thank you very much indeed for such an attractive, thrilled and heart punching 'Truth for the

TRUTH FOR THE JOURNEY

Journey,' really encouraging, meaningfully, significant, valuable and fabulous source of blessings for us. It is our prayer that the Lord may bless more effectively and use for His glory and honor and sprinkle His special anointing upon you and your entire team as well. God bless you."
Bishop Nasir Bashir Mall, Jr., The UMC Pakistan, Pakistan
(in response to "The Best School for Prayer is on our Knees," 31st May 2011)

"We appreciate your work that you are doing for the Lord Jesus. God bless you and use you abundantly for His glory."
Pastor Samson Daniel, Grace of God Ministries, Pakistan
(in response to "Unselfish & Unconditional LOVE," 1st July 2011)

"Great having your write up for this day. Quite full of deep insights. The LORD will increase your anointing more and more. Remain a blessed man that you are in the Lord. We love you."
Rev/Dr. Femi Success, The Word Cup, Nigeria
(in response to "We Overcome Satan, When we say (utter with our own mouths) What God says about the Blood..!" 9th July 2011)

"Thanks for the message. This is my rhema for today. I haven't been tithing for a long time due to insufficient cash. I believe this message has changed my life. Thanks."
John Theodore-Edevu
(in response to "True Prosperity is Linked to Tithing, Seed Sowing & Giving," 26th July 2011)

Drs Alan and Jennifer Pateman

Senior and Co-Apostles

Drs Alan and Jennifer Pateman, missionaries from the UK, who at present reside in Tuscany, Italy, and travel together as an apostolic couple. They are the Founders of Alan Pateman World Missions, Connecting for Excellence International, and LifeStyle International Christian University. President and Vice President of World Missions Ministries Association and APMI Publishing/Publications.

(Please see our website for all profile and international information, itinerant, conferences and graduations, etc.)

www.AlanPatemanWorldMissions.com

To Contact the Author

Please email:

Alan Pateman World Missions

Email: apostledr@alanpatemanworldmissions.com
Web: www.AlanPatemanWorldMissions.com

*Please include your prayer requests
and comments when you write.*

Other Books

Kingdom Dimensions– Being Triumphant over all our Insecurities

You'll find here practical wisdom, scriptural insights, and prayer that has helped many walk in victory. We will address topics like insecurity vs. security, competition, criticism, inability to trust, narcissism, self-indulgence, and the difficulty many have with receiving correction.

ISBN: 978-1-918102-03-1, Pages: 116,
Format: Paperback, Published: 2025
Also available in eBook format!

His Faith–Positions Us For Possession

It is with both simplicity and seasoned proficiency that Dr Pateman draws us into this weighty conclusion; …only as we yield and surrender to Christ's faith IN us – will we truly be empowered to live as Christ lived on this earth, "…as he is, so are we in this world" *(1 John 4:17).*

ISBN: 978-0-9570654-0-6, Pages: 128,
Format: Paperback, Published: 2014
Also available in eBook format!

ACADEMIC BRILLIANCE

JOIN OUR FAMILY OF EXCEPTIONAL STUDENTS AT
LIFESTYLE INTERNATIONAL CHRISTIAN UNIVERSITY

OFFERING UP TO 84% SCHOLARSHIP DISCOUNTS

FULL Scholarships available for students who bring 5 paying students on board! Covering all tuition fees (except for books, writing, and graduation fees). Valid for as long as the five students continue their monthly courses.

Registration is open

Helping to equip students for life and ministry with relevant studies.

Dr. Alan Pateman an Apostle, Bishop of World Missions and Connecting for Excellence International. He is also the Chancellor of LICU University.

INSPIRATIONAL & HOLY SPIRIT FILLED COURSES

Contact our office for more details!
www.licuuniversity.com
Tel. +39 366 329 1315

ALAN PATEMAN WORLD MISSIONS.COM

Join us
in Supporting the
GOSPEL
and the work and ministry of
Alan & Jennifer Pateman

BECOME A PATRON
FOR JUST €12 A MONTH

THANK YOU
FOR YOUR CONTINUOUS SUPPORT, WE ARE FAMILY

Patrons Benefits:
1) Patrons monthly news letter
2) Personal mentoring with Dr. Alan through WhatsApp and Prayer
3) Free Book every year
4) Teaching Courses for personal study
5) Free Conference every year
6) Free Patrons Dinner

Tel: 0039 366 329 1315

... for those who are Hungry to be Empowered

Copyright APMI Publications

All Books Available

at

APMI PUBLICATIONS

Email: publications@alanpatemanworldmissions.com
*Also Available from Amazon.com
and other retail outlets.*

If you purchased this book through Amazon.com or other and enjoyed reading it, or perhaps one of my other books, I would be grateful if you could take a couple of minutes to write a Customer Review, many thanks.

BY DR. ALAN PATEMAN

The Reality of a Warrior

La Realta del Guerriero *(Italian Translation)*

Healing and Deliverance, A Present Reality

Control, A Powerful Force

His Life is in the Blood

Sexual Madness, In a Sexually Confused World *(co-authored with Jennifer Pateman)*

Apostles, Can the Church Survive Without Them?

Prayer, Ingredients for Successful Intercession, Part One

Prayer, Touching the Heart of God, Part Two

The Early Years, Anointed Generals Past and Present, Part One of Four

Revival Fires, Anointed Generals Past and Present, Part Two of Four

Why War, A Biblical Approach to the Armour of God and Spiritual Warfare

Forgiveness, the Key to Revival

His Faith, Positions us for Possession

Seduction & Control: Infiltrating Society and the Church

Kingdom Management for Anointed Prosperity

TONGUES, our Supernatural Prayer Language

Seven Pillars for Life and Kingdom Prosperity

WINNING by Mastering your Mind

Laying Foundations

Apostles and the Local Church

Preparations for Ministry

Developments and Provision

The Age of Apostolic Apostleship

Media, Spiritual Gateway *(co-authored with Jennifer Pateman)*

Israel, the Question of Ownership

Earnestly Contending for the State of Israel

The Temple, Antichrist and the New World Order

The Antichrist, Rapture and the Battle of Armageddon

Israel, the Church and the End Times

Introduction to all things APMI

Student's Handbook, Study Guide Volume 2

Empowered to Overcome

Equipped for Spiritual Warfare

Appropriations of African Territory

China, Covid-19, World Domination

Watchers of the 4 Kings

Coronavirus – Communist and Marxist Uprising

Changing Worlds, The Great Reset Deception

Davos and the Great Reset

The Ukraine Conflict – Waking Up to a New World Order

God's Anointed Well Diggers	The Apostolic Reformation and Restoration
Campus Set Up Helper, Study Guide Volume 3	The Nature of the Apostolic
Campus Guideline Handbook, Study Guide Volume 4	The Triune God
	The Road to Maturity
Instructor's Handbook, Study Guide Volume 5	The Warrior's Garb
	The Warrior's Stance
The Fire of God that Gives us the Boldness to Break Free of Religion	Three Faces of Control
	Free to be Responsible
Power or Influence	Fantasy Explosion for the Heavy Viewer
Breaking Out, Financial Freedom	
God's Ways of Financial Increase	Breaking Free
The Wonders of Christmas	From Bondage to Freedom
Receiving Grace	Jezebel Influencing the Church
Eagles of Destiny ...a Prophetic Concept	New Age Seduction
The Breakthrough is found in His Presence *(31 Day Devotional)*	Marriage Under Threat
	The Controlling Syndrome
Excellent Conduct	My Biography
Kingdom Embrace	The Python Spirit is Sent to Strangle our Success
Believing in Kingdom Authority	
By Your Consent	The Power of Deliverance
Living in His Overcoming Faith	Please, I Have a Question
The Culture of HONOUR	Prophetic Trumpets and he that Overcomes
Truth for the Journey	
I Need You, HOLY SPIRIT	Kingdom Dimensions–Being Triumphant over all our Insecurities

BY DR. JENNIFER PATEMAN

Sexual Madness, In a Sexually Confused World *(co-authored with Alan Pateman)*	What comes first the Chicken or the Egg?
	Writing Guidelines for Research Papers, Study Guide Volume 6
Millennial Myopia, From a Biblical Perspective	
	Writing Guidelines for Bachelor and Master Theses, Study Guide Volume 7
Media, Spiritual Gateway *(co-authored with Alan Pateman)*	
	Writing Guidelines for Doctoral Dissertations, Study Guide Volume 8
Truth Endures to All Generations	

AVAILABLE FROM APMI PUBLICATIONS, AMAZON.COM AND OTHER RETAIL OUTLETS

www.ingramcontent.com/pod-product-compliance
Lightning Source LLC
Chambersburg PA
CBHW070723160426
43192CB00009B/1294